W9-AXR-292

The
Osteoporosis Prevention Guide

The
Osteoporosis Prevention Guide

❧❧❧

The natural strategy for strengthening your bones

DR. SARAH BREWER

BARNES
&NOBLE
BOOKS
NEW YORK

1999 Barnes & Noble Books

ISBN 0-7607-1184-4 *casebound*
ISBN 0-7607-1185-2 *paperback*

Printed and bound in the United States of America

99 00 01 02 MC 9 8 7 6 5 4 3 2 1
99 00 01 02 MP 9 8 7 6 5 4 3 2 1

FG

Contents

Note to Readers   6

1   An Introduction to Osteoporosis   7
2   General Measures for Preventing Osteoporosis   11
3   Exercises to Help Strengthen Your Bones   28
4   Diet and Osteoporosis   42
5   Vitamins and Minerals for Bone Health   57
6   Osteoporosis Prevention During Pregnancy   82
7   Complementary Treatments to Help Strengthen
        Your Bones   89
8   Bone-Building Recipes   106
9   Prevention and Treatment with Drugs   150

Appendices   165
Foods High in Calcium   167
Foods High in Magnesium   170
Foods High in Zinc   173
Foods High in Vitamin D   174
Optimum Healthy Weight Range   176
Your Personal Osteoporosis Risk Analysis   179
Useful Addresses   184

Index   189

Note to Readers

Every care has been taken to ensure that the instructions and advice given in this book are accurate and practical. However, where health is concerned – and in particular a serious problem of any kind – it must be stressed that there is no substitute for seeking advice from a qualified medical practitioner. All persistent symptoms, of whatever nature, may have underlying causes that need, and should not be treated without, professional elucidation and evaluation. It is therefore very important, if you intend to use this book for self-help, only to do so in conjunction with duly prescribed conventional or other therapy. In any event, read the advice carefully, and pay particular attention to the precautions and warnings.

The Publisher makes no representation, express or implied, with regard to the accuracy of the information contained in this book, and legal responsibility or liability cannot be accepted by the Author or the Publisher for any errors or omissions that may be made or for any loss, damage, injury or problems suffered or in any way arising from following the advice offered in these pages.

CHAPTER 1

An Introduction to Osteoporosis

Osteoporosis is so common that it has been described as the silent epidemic. More than three million people in the UK are affected, and between seven and eight million in the USA, yet it is largely a preventable disease. While bone thinning is a normal part of the ageing process, you can significantly reduce your risk of brittle bones by ensuring that they are as strong as possible before they start to erode. The denser your bones are in youth, the less likely they are to thin down below the level at which fractures occur in later life. Increasing your bone strength by as little as 10 per cent in middle age can halve your risk of a fracture in later years. This means that, even if you have a family tendency towards osteoporosis, it need not necessarily cause problems in the future.

WHAT IS OSTEOPOROSIS?

Your bones are a living tissue made up of a network of collagen fibres filled with mineral salts. These minerals—of which the most important is calcium phosphate—are in a constant state of flux, with some cells constantly building up new bone while others dissolve old, worn-out bone. Researchers now know that osteoporosis develops when this remodelling activity becomes unbalanced so that too much bone is absorbed and not enough laid down. This causes bones to thin, become brittle and fracture more easily. Research shows that several diet and lifestyle changes can help you build up stronger bones and even reverse the thinning process, so that your risk of osteoporosis is reduced.

Whether you are fit and healthy or already suffering from osteoporosis, the bone-building plan contained in this book can help to strengthen your bones and reduce your future risk of a fracture. Osteoporosis prevention means:

- Eating a healthy, balanced diet full of calcium and other bone-building nutrients such as magnesium, phosphate, potassium, zinc and vitamin C. A high intake of fruit and vegetables has recently been shown to protect against osteoporosis.
- Getting all the vitamins you need from your food—especially vitamin D which is also made in your skin during sensible exposure to sunlight.
- Obtaining essential fatty acids from nuts, seeds, oily fish and dark green leafy vegetables, or by taking supplements such as evening primrose and fish oils. Essential fatty acids have been shown to increase absorption of calcium from your gut, increase the amount of calcium laid down in your bones and reduce the amount lost through your kidneys.
- Taking regular exercise—especially activities that are high impact in nature (e.g. aerobics, gymnastics, netball, dancing, racquet sports, jogging, skipping), although brisk walking is also beneficial. Exercise stimulates the laying down of new bone, especially in areas where slight weakness is detected by bone cells (osteoclasts).
- Stopping smoking—smoking cigarettes damps down formation of new bone and reduces oestrogen hormone levels. If you are a smoker, this is one of the most important lifestyle changes you can make for your total health, not just that of your bones.
- Avoiding *excessive* alcohol intake which reduces absorp-

tion of dietary calcium from your gut and is linked with early osteoporosis. Moderate alcohol intake, however, may increase bone density and reduce the risk of osteoporosis. The exact mechanism remains unclear but it is reassuring that social drinking is unlikely to be harmful to bones.

- Avoiding heavy consumption of coffee, meat and salt which are linked with early osteoporosis.
- Taking especial care with your diet during pregnancy and when breast-feeding. As well as giving your baby the best possible start in life, this will help keep your bones strong at a time when any dietary deficiency means that calcium and other nutrients will be leached from your bones to ensure that your developing baby does not go without.
- Considering taking hormone replacement therapy (HRT) if you are a woman who is experiencing menopausal symptoms or are post-menopausal.
- Taking supplements containing oestrogenic and progestogenic herbs if you are unable or unwilling to take HRT.

Some people have an extra-high risk of developing osteoporosis and should start preventative measures as soon as possible. These include:

Women who:
- have had an early menopause (under 45 years of age);
- have had a hysterectomy, especially if accompanied by removal of both ovaries;
- have had periods that stopped (amenorrhoea) for any cause except pregnancy (e.g. excessive dieting, excessive exercise, use of depot progestogen, the contraceptive injection).

Men who:
- have reduced levels of male sex hormones due to under-functioning of the testicles (hypogonadism);
- exercise excessively, e.g. marathon runners, exercise trainers.

Men and women who:
- have a close family history of osteoporosis;
- have regularly used oral corticosteroids for three months or longer;
- smoke heavily;
- drink excessive amounts of alcohol;
- have lost a lot of weight, or who are naturally very thin (body mass index less than 20 calculated from weight in kilograms divided by height in metres then divided by height in metres again):

$$\text{BMI} = \frac{weight \ (kg)}{height \times height \ (M^2)}$$

e.g. someone weighing 50 kg who is 1.6m tall has a BMI of $50/1.6/1.6 = 19.5\text{kg/M}^2$;

- have a poor diet providing low intakes of vitamins and minerals, especially calcium, magnesium, phosphorus and vitamin D;
- have a history of prolonged bed rest, especially in childhood;
- are housebound with little exposure to sunlight and with low dietary intakes of vitamin D and calcium;
- have liver problems;
- have overactive parathyroid glands (hyperparathyroidism) or an overactive thyroid gland (hyperthyroidism).

It is never too early or too late to take preventative measures against the silent epidemic. Even if you are already a sufferer, you can help to prevent your condition becoming worse. This book will show you how.

CHAPTER 2

General Measures for Preventing Osteoporosis

Your diet and lifestyle are so important to hormone balance that stopping smoking and improving nutrition can delay the menopause by as much as three or four years. They can also delay, minimise or even prevent the onset of osteoporosis. It has been shown, for example, that women who reach the menopause and do not smoke (or stop smoking) and who keep their alcohol intake to within recommended limits, have a 40 per cent lower risk of a hip fracture than a woman who smokes and drinks alcohol to excess.

SUNLIGHT

Although excessive sun is harmful, sensible exposure is necessary to help prevent osteoporosis. Your skin contains a cholesterol-like molecule which interacts with sunlight to produce vitamin D (calciferol). Only ultraviolet light of a certain wavelength can trigger this reaction (290nm–310nm) and this is mostly missing from British sunlight between the end of October and the end of March. Blood levels of vitamin D are therefore naturally higher in the summer and lower in winter. For the remainder of the year, these wavelengths occur mainly between 11.00 am and 3.00 pm, and are readily blocked by clouds.

Vitamin D is essential for healthy bones and teeth as it is

needed for the absorption of dietary calcium and phosphate from the small intestines (see p.78). People who live in high altitudes, cover up their skin in sunlight or who stay indoors all day, are not exposed to enough sunlight to meet their vitamin D needs naturally. They must therefore rely on getting vitamin D from their diet. Just going without sunlight exposure for six weeks can deplete your vitamin D stores enough to reduce the amount of calcium you can absorb from your food. Lack of vitamin D during childhood can lead to deformed bones (rickets), while in adults it causes weakened, softened bones (osteomalacia) and increases the risk of osteoporosis.

To help prevent osteoporosis:

- go outside every day to get some fresh air;
- just 15 minutes' exposure to bright sunshine on your face is enough to generate your vitamin D needs during the summer—but during winter you will need at least 30 minutes' exposure to daylight for the same benefit;
- dark-skinned people need more sun exposure than those who are fair-skinned to meet their vitamin D needs.

Research suggests that baring your arms, face and legs to 30 minutes of sunshine per day—but without burning—is as beneficial for your bones as increasing your dietary vitamin D intake by a factor of four. By exercising while you are outside enjoying the fresh air, you can more than double the beneficial effects of being outdoors. For information on foods containing vitamin D, see chapter 5.

ALCOHOL

A moderate intake of alcohol—especially red wine—can be beneficial for health generally by reducing stress levels and lowering your risk of high blood pressure, coronary heart disease and stroke by up to 40 per cent compared with a teetotaller. Fortunately, a moderate intake of alcohol is also beneficial for female bones, although excessive alcohol will increase your risk of osteoporosis.

Moderate alcohol intake and bones

Research shows that post-menopausal women who drink three glasses of wine a day (or two drinks of hard liquor or three beers) have a bone density that is 5–10 per cent greater than in non-drinkers, regardless of age, weight, height, smoking habits or whether they take hormone replacement therapy. No such beneficial effects on bone have been found for men, however. The mechanism remains unclear, but researchers have suggested that this intake of alcohol may improve bone mineral density by increasing oestrogen levels in women, while it lowers testosterone levels in men.

In fact, one study has suggested that men who drink moderately may actually have more than double the risk of osteoporosis compared with male teetotallers.

Sensible drinking advice is that:

● men should aim to drink no more than 3–4 units of alcohol per day, with an average weekly intake of 28 units considered not to cause a significant health risk;
● women should drink no more than 2–3 units per day, with an average weekly limit of 21 units.

1 unit of alcohol is equivalent to:
—100ml (1 glass) of wine *or*
—50ml (one measure) of sherry *or*
—25ml (one tot) of spirit *or*
—300ml (half a pint) of normal strength beer.

Most people tend to overestimate the strength of spirits and underestimate the strength of beer:

● someone drinking two pints of beer has consumed FOUR units.

- someone drinking two glasses of wine and a double vodka has also consumed FOUR units.

Excessive alcohol intake and bones

Excessive alcohol is harmful to your general health (heart disease, liver disease) and increases your risk of osteoporosis by:

- increasing your risk of malnourishment and lack of vitamins and minerals;
- inhibiting absorption of bone-building nutrients such as vitamin C, folic acid, calcium, copper, magnesium and zinc;
- increasing excretion of minerals such as calcium which are leached from bone;
- generating free radicals which damage bone cells, and lowering levels of vitamin C;
- affecting vitamin D metabolism;
- increasing your risk of indigestion so that you are more likely to consume aluminium-containing antacids that affect bone phosphorus and calcium balance;
- having a direct toxic effect against bone cells;
- lowering testosterone hormone levels in men.

Excessive alcohol seems to reduce absorption of dietary calcium from the gut and is linked with low bone mass and early osteoporosis. You can help to prevent brittle bones by ensuring your intake is within the recommended safe maximum. Women who stop smoking and drinking at the time of the menopause may reduce their risk of a fracture by as much as 40 per cent.

For men, drinking more than 50 units of alcohol per week is considered dangerous, while for women, the equivalent figure is 35 units.

If you drink more than the recommended maximum, it is important that you cut back. Simple tips to help you reduce your alcohol intake include:

- sipping slowly and putting your glass down each time rather than holding it in your hand—this will reduce the amount you sip by habit, when talking;
- savouring each sip and holding it in your mouth for longer;
- mixing chilled white or red wine with sparkling mineral water to make a refreshing spritzer;
- alternating each alcoholic drink with a non-alcoholic one;
- drinking mineral water with a dash of fresh lemon juice, or low-calorie drinks;
- trying exotic, non-alcoholic cocktails—e.g. mango juice with coconut milk;
- substituting tonic water with ice, lemon and a dash of Angostura bitters for a gin and tonic;
- substituting elderflower cordial diluted with mineral water for white wine;
- drinking fruit or herbal teas.

Could you be drinking too much alcohol?
If you are not sure whether you are drinking within sensible limits, keep a careful alcohol diary each week and analyse it to see how much you are actually drinking.

The following simple, screening questionnaire (the CAGE questionnaire) has been designed by drinking experts to help alert you to a possible drinking problem. If you answer YES to two or more questions, you may have an alcohol problem— see your doctor for advice as soon as possible.

- Do you ever feel you should cut down on your drinking?
- Are you ever annoyed by people criticising your drinking?
- Do you ever feel guilty about your drinking?
- Do you ever drink first thing in the morning?

Another useful questionnaire devised by drinking experts in the United States (the BMAST questionnaire), helps to detect signs of alcohol addiction. Answer YES or NO to each of the following ten questions and add up your scores in the columns.

A score of six or more points indicates you may suffer from alcohol addiction. Seek advice from your doctor straight away.

	YES	NO
Do you feel you are a NORMAL drinker?	0	2
Do friends or relatives think you are a NORMAL drinker?	0	2
Have you ever lost friends because of your drinking?	2	0
Have you been in trouble at work/college or school through drink?	2	0
Have you ever neglected family, work or obligations for two or more days in a row through drink?	2	0
Have you ever sought help about your alcoholic intake?	5	0
Have you ever visited Alcoholics Anonymous?	5	0
Have you ever had the shakes (DTs), heard voices or seen things that weren't there?	5	0
Have you ever been to hospital because of drinking?	5	0
Have you ever been arrested for drink/driving or failed a breathalyser test?	2	0

Total =

SMOKING

Smoking cigarettes significantly increases your risk of osteoporosis. It lowers blood oestrogen levels and, in women, can trigger a premature menopause up to five years earlier than normal. Smoking also reduces the activity of bone-building cells (osteoblasts) so that less new bone is made. Recent research shows that one in eight hip fractures in women is due to smoking. This showed that:

- for women aged 60, smokers were 17 per cent more likely than non-smokers to suffer a hip fracture;
- at 70 years, smokers were 41 per cent more likely to have a hip fracture;
- at 80 years, smokers were 71 per cent more likely to have a hip fracture;
- at 90 years, smokers were 10 per cent more likely to have a hip fracture than non-smokers.

Little difference in hip fracture rate was noticed in pre-menopausal women, however. By stopping smoking and improving her diet, a woman can expect to delay her menopause by at least three or four years—and help to reduce her future risk of osteoporosis. Stopping smoking also has other major benefits in reducing risk of a variety of other diseases such as coronary heart disease and cancer, such that, on average, non-smokers live six years longer than smokers.

Stopping smoking has immediate health benefits for your bones and preventing osteoporosis:

Within 20 minutes: Your blood pressure and pulse fall significantly to improve your general circulation, including blood flow to your bones.

Within 8 hours: Levels of poisonous carbon monoxide in the blood reaching your bones fall and blood oxygen levels increase to normal.

Within 48 hours: The level of clotting factors in your blood reduces to normal so that blood is less sticky and circulation through tiny capillaries in bones is improved.

Within 1–3 months: Improvements in your general circulation, including that in bone, are maximised.

Within 5 years: adverse effects of smoking on collagen formation disappear.

Tips on how to stop smoking
Nicotine is addictive and giving up smoking takes a lot of commitment. Try the following quit plan:

- Name the day to give up and get into the right frame of mind beforehand.
- Try to stop at the same time as a friend or relative for support.
- Throw away all your cigarettes and spare packets.
- Throw away all smoking bits and pieces such as cigarette papers, matches, lighters and ashtrays.
- Take it one day at a time—the thought of never smoking again is daunting, so just concentrate on getting through each day.
- Keep a chart and tick off each successful cigarette-free day.
- Find something to occupy your hands to help break the hand-to-mouth habit, e.g. make models, paint, draw, learn origami or make straw dollies.
- Take extra exercise which stimulates release of brain chemicals that help to curb nicotine cravings.
- Keep active with DIY jobs in the evening rather than sitting in front of the TV.
- Avoid situations where you used to smoke.
- Learn to say, 'No thanks, I've given up', and mean it.
- Ask friends and relatives not to smoke around you.
- Plan a reward for every week of cigarette-free success, e.g. join a health club with the money you've saved.

When you have an urge to smoke, try:

- sucking on an artificial cigarette or herbal stick available in chemist shops;
- sucking on celery or carrot sticks;
- eating an apple;
- cleaning your teeth with strong-flavoured toothpaste;

- going out for a brisk walk, swim, cycle-ride or jog;
- taking a supplement containing oat straw (*Avena sativa*) which can reduce cravings.

An aromatherapy device impregnated with 19 essential oils (Logado, available from chemists) can be sniffed or inhaled so that cigarette cravings disappear for up to 30 minutes. To non-smokers, the device smells like an old ashtray, but to smokers it is a delicious combination of tobacco and aromatic scents that make you feel as if you've just had a cigarette. The aromatherapy scents help to relax you and also block your sense of smell—so even if you do smoke, the cigarette will taste insipid. In trials, one in three smokers using Logado regularly gave up, and a further one in four cut the amount they smoked by half. (UK Logado Consumer Advice Line: 01223 426410.)

Nicotine replacement therapy (gum, patches, nasal sprays, inhaler) can help, too. Studies show that nicotine replacement therapy can double the chance of successfully giving up smoking. Don't be tempted to smoke while using nicotine replacement therapy, however, as this can trigger spasm of blood vessels which reduces blood flow to all tissues in your body—including your bones, heart and brain—and can be dangerous.

If withdrawal symptoms are particularly strong, try the following breathing exercise to help reduce your stress levels:

- Breathe in slowly and deeply.
- When you reach your limit of breathing in, immediately start to breath out—without holding your breath—to empty your lungs as much as possible.
- Repeat five times without holding your breath in between.

ALUMINIUM ANTACIDS

Avoid using aluminium-containing antacids if you suffer from indigestion or heartburn. Long-term exposure to aluminium increases your risk of osteoporosis by interfering with calcium absorption from the gut, reducing deposition of calcium in bone and reducing collagen formation to weaken the bone matrix. Ideally, you should also stop using aluminium saucepans or at least avoid cooking acidic foods such as rhubarb in them. This is because rhubarb interacts with the aluminium oxide on the surface of the pan to dissolve it (and makes the pan go shiny). When rhubarb was cooked in a stainless steel pan, it contained 0.1mg aluminium per portion. When cooked in an aluminium pan, it contained 250 times as much (25mg per portion).

STRESS

Excess stress has recently been linked with more severe symptoms during the menopause, and with an increased risk of osteoporosis in women. By taking steps to reduce your stress levels, you can help to prevent future osteoporosis. The reason seems to be due to the adrenal glands, which are responsible for producing stress hormones such as cortisol and adrenaline but which can also produce sex hormones.

Usually, up to 5 per cent of circulating sex hormones are made by your adrenal glands. As the ovaries shut down during the menopause, the adrenal glands usually provide some back-up by producing small amounts of oestrogen and doubling their output of testosterone-like male hormones (androgens). If you are under long-term stress, however, your adrenal glands may already be working flat out producing stress hormones such as adrenaline. When your menopause approaches, they have no extra reserves to boost their output of sex hormones. Stressed women therefore tend to suffer more and worse menopausal symptoms than women who are more in control of their life, and have an increased risk of osteoporosis.

Stress hormones also have a direct harmful effect on bone— cortisol, for example, has been shown to increase calcium resorption from bone and to increase calcium loss in the urine.

Are you suffering from stress?

The physical symptoms of stress can include:

tiredness	trembling
sweating	pins and needles
flushing	numbness
nausea	headache
insomnia	chest pain
palpitations	stomach pain
rapid pulse	diarrhoea
dizziness	period problems
faintness	

The emotional symptoms of stress can include:

- loss of concentration;
- being unable to make decisions;
- a tendency to become vague and forgetful;
- over-defensiveness and inability to take criticism;
- extreme anger;
- overwhelming feelings of anxiety and panic;
- fear of failure or rejection;
- feelings of guilt and shame;
- negative thoughts;
- moodiness;
- loss of sex drive and sexual problems;
- obsessive or compulsive behaviour;
- feelings of isolation;
- a feeling of impending doom.

The behavioural symptoms of stress can include:

- compulsive eating habits;
- excessive use of alcohol or tobacco;
- abuse of drugs;
- avoidance of places or situations;
- increased aggression;
- change in sleeping habits, particularly early wakening.

By keeping a stress diary you can monitor the causes of stress in your life. Try to fill in your diary immediately after each stressful event—don't leave it until later or you will not remember exactly how you felt. For example:

DATE	TIME	SITUATION	FEELINGS	RESPONSE	FUTURE REMEDY
	8.00	Overslept	Dreadful	No breakfast	Set back-up snooze alarm
	9.30	Late for work	Worried	Drove too fast	
	13.00	Stuck in traffic on way to meeting	Frustrated, panicky	Tried classical music and deep breathing	Leave in plenty of time
	18.00	Supermarket crowded	Hot and flustered	Rushed out forgetting to buy some things	Shop when store quieter

At the end of a week go back over your diary and try to identify your main sources of stress, how much control you have over them and which situations can be changed or improved. Think about your habits and consider whether any are making things worse. For example, do you always allow insufficient time to drive to meetings? Do you always leave things to the last minute so that you run out of time? Do you always shop on a Friday evening when the supermarket is unbearable?

Coping with stress

The best way to cope with stress is to adapt to it in a positive, constructive manner. Situations must be seen in perspective, problems analysed logically and plans made to resolve them. By changing the way you look on a situation, you can reduce the amount of stress it causes. By thinking more positively, you can also improve your self-esteem. If you catch yourself thinking a negative thought, quickly turn it into a positive one. For example,

- 'I'm not very good at my job' becomes 'I AM good at my job'.
- 'I can't do this' becomes 'I CAN deal with this problem'.
- 'I can't cope if this happens' becomes 'I've coped with worse in the past'.
- 'This is too difficult' becomes 'This challenge will help me learn new skills'.
- 'I made a mistake' becomes 'I will learn from this experience so I don't do it again'.

Breathing exercises

The following breathing exercise will help to control the effects of stress and reduce your feelings of panic:

- Sit back in your chair or car seat.
- Drop and widen your shoulders by relaxing your arms.
- Expand your chest and fill your lungs as far as possible, then breathe out as completely as you can, being aware of the rise and fall of your abdomen—not your chest.
- Repeat five times without holding your breath in between.
- Continue to breathe regularly, getting your rhythm right by counting from 1–3 when breathing in and from 1–4 on breathing out.

When you feel panic building up inside:

- Say 'STOP' quietly to yourself.
- Breathe out deeply, then breathe in slowly.
- Hold this breath for a count of three and breathe out gently, letting the tension go.
- Continue to breathe regularly, imagining a feather floating in front of your face. As you breathe the feather should sway gently but not blow away.
- Continue breathing gently and consciously try to relax— let your tense muscles unwind and try to speak and move more slowly.

Stretch exercises to relieve stress

Try the following when you need a quick break from your desk, or as a general energiser after a long day:

Arm-swinging

- Stand up and take a few deep breaths.
- Stretch both arms in front of you at shoulder height.
- Let your arms relax and drop to your sides, let them swing to a standstill. Repeat several times.
- Finally, raise your arms above your shoulders and swing energetically.

Hand-shaking

- Shake each hand and arm in turn for a minute or two.
- When you stop, your muscles will feel soft and re-laxed.
- Repeat, using your legs and feet if you wish.

Relaxing your neck

- Imagine you are carrying a heavy weight in each hand so that your shoulders are pulled towards the floor.
- Drop the weight and feel the tension release. Repeat several times and feel your neck become less tense.

Circling your shoulders

- Circle your left shoulder in a backward direction five times. Repeat with right shoulder.
- Circle your left shoulder in a forward direction five times. Repeat with right shoulder.
- Repeat circling both shoulders together.

General relaxation

Having a bath or sit quietly for an hour, reading a book or magazine. Use an aromatherapy diffuser to fill the air with the scent of a relaxing essential oil. Have a candle-lit bath to which you have added one or more of the following anti-stress aromatherapy oils diluted in a carrier oil:

basil*	grapefruit
bergamot	jasmine*
cardamom	lavender*
cedarwood*	marjoram*
chamomile Roman	neroli
clary-sage*	rose
coriander	rosewood
cypress*	sandalwood
fennel	vetiver
geranium*	

*Do not use during pregnancy without seeking advice from a qualified practitioner.

Deep relaxation

For a deep relaxation exercise which tenses and relaxes different muscle groups to relieve tension, set aside at least half an hour. This exercise is especially beneficial after a long soak in a warm bath.

Find somewhere quiet and warm to lie down. Remove your shoes and loosen tight clothing. Close your eyes and keep them closed throughout the session.

First, lift your **forearms** into the air, bending them at the elbow. Clench your **fists** hard and concentrate on the tension in these muscles.

Breathe in deeply and slowly. As you breathe out, start to relax and let the tension in your arms drain away. Release your clenched fists and lower your arms gently down beside you. Feel the tension flow out of them until your fingers start to tingle. Your arms may start to feel as if they don't belong to you. Keep breathing gently and slowly.

Now tense your **shoulders and neck**, shrugging your shoulders up as high as you can. Feel the tension in your head, shoulders, neck and chest. Hold it for a moment. Then, slowly let the tension flow away. Breathe gently and slowly as the tension flows away.

Now lift your *head* up and push it forwards. Feel the tension in your neck. Tighten all your *facial muscles*. Clench your teeth, frown and screw up your eyes. Feel the tension on your face, the tightness in your skin and jaw, the wrinkles on your brow. Hold this tension for a few seconds, then start to relax. Let go gradually, concentrating on each set of muscles as they relax. A feeling of warmth will spread across your head as the tension is released. Your head will feel heavy and very relaxed.

Continue in this way, working next on your *back* muscles (providing you don't have a back problem) by pulling your shoulders and head backwards and arching your back upwards. Hold this for a few moments before letting your weight sink comfortably down as you relax. Check that your arms, head and neck are still relaxed, too.

Pull in your *abdomen* as tightly as you can. Then, as you breathe out, slowly release and feel the tension drain away. Now blow out your stomach as if tensing against a blow. Hold this tension for a few moments, then slowly relax.

Make sure tension has not crept back into parts of your body you have already relaxed. Your upper body should feel heavy, calm and relaxed.

Now, concentrate on your *legs*. Pull your *toes* up towards you and feel the tightness down the front of your legs. Push your toes away from you and feel the tightness spread up your legs. Hold this for a few moments, then lift your legs into the air, either together or one at a time. Hold for a few moments and then lower your legs until they are at rest.

Relax your thighs, buttocks, calves and feet. Let them flop under their own weight and relax. Feel the tension flow down your legs and out through your toes. Feel your legs become heavy and relaxed. Your toes may tingle.

Your whole body should now feel very heavy and very

relaxed. Breathe calmly and slowly and feel all that tension drain away.

Imagine you are lying in a warm, sunny meadow with a stream bubbling gently beside you. Relax for at least twenty minutes, occasionally checking your body for tension.

In your own time bring the session to a close.

CHAPTER 3

Exercises to Help Strengthen Your Bones

Regular exercise has a strengthening effect and can help to prevent osteoporosis. Your bones respond to the mechanical pressures applied to them so that areas under stress become thicker and stronger. Regular weight-bearing exercise therefore helps to build up your bones by putting pressure on them, as well as increasing muscle strength. Research with professional tennis players, for example, shows the bones in their racquet-holding arm are thicker than on the other side. Conversely, lack of exercise and immobility (e.g. through wearing a plaster cast or being bedridden) cause bones to thin down. Astronauts living in space, who lose the effects of gravity and weight on their bones, have also been shown to lose as much as 200mg of calcium from their bones per day.

Luckily, these effects are reversible, and starting a regular exercise regime can help to re-strengthen bones and reduce the risk of osteoporosis. When a group of post-menopausal women were started on an exercise regime consisting of 5–10 minutes' stretching followed by 30 minutes' walking, jogging or dance routines three times a week for one year, their bones were found to be significantly stronger than in a non-exercising control group.

EXERCISES TO HELP STRENGTHEN YOUR BONES

How exercise builds up bone
Bones contain a network of cells (osteocytes and osteoblasts) that connect with each other through fine strands of tissue. When bone is stressed, these strands are stretched, pulled, compressed and twisted, too. This acts as a signal to stimulate production of new bone in these areas, so bone mass increases locally at the sites where bone is under greatest stress. The rate at which new bone forms depends on the size and speed of the force the bone is subjected to. The higher the force and the faster it is applied, the greater the rate at which new bone is made; if the force is too great, however, the bone may bend enough to break.

Exercise also stimulates blood circulation so that more oxygen and nutrients such as calcium reach your bones. Studies have shown that exercise strengthens bone in pre-menopausal and post-menopausal women and in men.

By strengthening your muscles and improving your stamina, suppleness and balance, regular exercise also reduces the likelihood of a fall in older people. Together with the bone-strengthening effect of exercise, this decreases the risk of sustaining an osteoporotic bone fracture. In contrast, physical inactivity greatly increases the chance of a hip fracture.

What sort of exercise is best?
The forces that act on your bones to stimulate thickening include:

- traction which stretches the bone;
- compression which squashes the bone;
- bending which flexes the bone;
- torsion which twists the bone.

Weight-bearing activities that stress your bones in all these ways are most beneficial for strengthening them. These are generally high impact in nature such as:

aerobics	racquet sports
gymnastics	jogging
netball	running
dancing	skipping

In some studies, though not in all, brisk walking has also been shown to be beneficial.

Non-weight-bearing exercises such as swimming can also have a beneficial effect on bones as the muscle movements that bend your joints and flex your back also stress your bones slightly. Swimmers who do not take part in other types of competitive sport have been found to have greater bone mass in their forearms and back than non-athletes, for example.

Strength stamina and suppleness
After the menopause, your body will change in a number of ways:

- your bone density will fall by an average of 2–3 per cent per year;
- your strength will reduce by around 1–2 per cent per year;
- your power (strength × speed) will reduce by 3–4 per cent per year.

Different types of exercise can help to reduce these changes and in some cases prevent them all together. A study in which a group of women (aged 53–74 years) with mild osteoporosis were given bone-loading exercises to perform for 50 minutes, three times a week, found that bone density increased by 4 per cent over the course of a year. In contrast, a similar group of women who did not do these exercises continued to lose bone at a rate of up to 3 per cent over the same period. If exercise stops, however, bone mass will slowly fall again, so it is important to maintain your level of physical activity for sustained benefit.

EXERCISES TO HELP STRENGTHEN YOUR BONES

How often?

To achieve a steady gain in bone density, you need to take part in some form of weight-bearing exercise every day. The amount of exercise need not be particularly high—for example, you would gain a significant bone-loading benefit from just the equivalent of jumping up and down between 10 and 30 times per day.

Healthy exercise guidelines suggest that, ideally, you should aim to exercise at moderate intensity for 20–30 minutes five times a week. Your half-hour of exercise doesn't have to be completed all in one go—you can divide it into two or three daily sessions of 10–15 minutes if you prefer. Once you are fit, you should try to do some form of exercise every day.

Exercise is important for bone-strengthening in childhood, too, and children should be encouraged to take a minimum of two hours' exercise per week, preferably divided over two or more sessions.

Those over 70 will benefit from any general increase in their level of physical activity. Even standing rather than sitting or lying helps to strengthen bones, and activities such as walking, climbing stairs, carrying loads, doing housework, dancing, DIY and gardening have all been shown to help protect against osteoporotic fractures. This is true even when there are other risk factors for bone-thinning such as cigarette smoking and high-alcohol consumption. It is therefore important for the elderly to maintain their level of physical activity as much as possible.

What types of exercise should I choose?

Different types of exercise have different effects on your strength, stamina and suppleness:

THE OSTEOPOROSIS PREVENTION GUIDE

ACTIVITY	STRENGTH	STAMINA	SUPPLENESS	BONE DENSITY
Aerobics	**	***	***	****
Athletics	***	***	**	****
Badminton	**	**	***	****
Circuit training	***	***	***	***
Cricket	*	*	**	***
Cycling	***	****	**	*
Dancing	**	****	***	****
Football	***	***	***	***
Jogging	**	****	**	****
Netball	***	****	***	****
Skipping	**	***	**	****
Squash	**	***	***	****
Swimming (hard)	****	****	****	*
Tennis	**	**	***	****
Walking (brisk/hill)	**	***	*	**
Yoga	*	*	***	*

* = slight effect   *** = very good effect
** = beneficial effect   **** = excellent effect

Research in which women aged 35–45 years regularly took part in high impact exercise (jumping or step aerobics) for 18 months showed that their bone mineral density increased by a massive 14 to 37 per cent. This type of regular activity requires a high degree of commitment to reap the benefits, however. It is best to choose a type of activity that you enjoy and which you are likely to continue, than to start a demanding regime that you are unlikely to keep up.

Choose an activity to suit you
Exercise should be an enjoyable part of your life that you look forward to every day. If you prefer exercising alone, choose:

● walking—especially brisk or hill walking;
● cycling;
● a home gym work-out;

EXERCISES TO HELP STRENGTHEN YOUR BONES

- jogging;
- gardening.

If you prefer companionable exercise, choose:

- walking a dog;
- golf;
- bowling;
- table tennis;
- a work-out at a sports gym;
- an aerobics class;
- a dancing class;
- a keep-fit class;
- tennis or badminton;
- a rambling club;
- a team sport such as netball, volleyball, ladies' football, rounders, cricket or hockey.

If you need motivation or someone to direct you, choose:

- a home exercise video;
- an aerobics class;
- a personal trainer;
- an exercise class at a sports centre;
- an exercise organised by a club.

Choose a time to suit you

It is important that your chosen form of exercise can fit into your daily routine as you are then most likely to keep it up. This may be:

- early morning before setting off for work;
- on your way to or from work (e.g. walking part of the way);
- in your lunch hour;
- after work;
- in the early evening—only do light exercise (such as walking round the block with the dog) before going to bed, otherwise it may interfere with sleep.

How to start

If you are unfit, start slowly and build up the time and effort you spend on exercise.

- Always warm up first with a few simple bends and stretches.
- Cool down afterwards by walking slowly for a few minutes.
- Wear loose clothing and proper footwear specifically designed for the job and use any recommended safety equipment.
- Don't exercise straight after a heavy meal, after drinking alcohol or if you feel unwell.
- Stop immediately if you feel dizzy, faint, unusually short of breath or develop chest pain.

NB: People with established osteoporosis need to seek medical advice before starting an exercise programme, as placing extra strain on thin bones may increase your risk of a fracture. Similarly, if you are under medical supervision for a health problem—especially a heart condition—you should seek your doctor's advice before embarking on a regular exercise regime.

Suggested regime to walk yourself fit over three months

WEEK	TUESDAY	THURSDAY	SATURDAY	SUNDAY
1	10 mins	10 mins	10 mins	
2	10 mins	10 mins	10 mins	
3	10 mins	15 mins	10 mins	15 mins
4	15 mins	15 mins	15 mins	15 mins
5	15 mins	15 mins	15 mins	15 mins
6	15 mins	20 mins	15 mins	20 mins
7	20 mins	20 mins	20 mins	20 mins
8	20 mins	20 mins	20 mins	20 mins
9	20 mins	25 mins	20 mins	25 mins
10	25 mins	25 mins	25 mins	25 mins
11	25 mins	30 mins	25 mins	30 mins
12	30 mins	30 mins	30 mins	30 mins

EXERCISES TO HELP STRENGTHEN YOUR BONES

To maintain your new fitness level, try to obtain at least 30 minutes' exercise three times per week.

Tips to help you exercise more

- Take up an active hobby such as ballroom dancing, bowls, swimming, golf, walking or cycling.
- If you dislike exercise, try to put more effort into DIY or gardening.
- Spend less time watching TV and more time pottering in the garden or around the house—listen to music or the radio if you like background noise.
- Borrow a dog and take it for regular walks.
- Walk up stairs rather than using the lift or escalator.
- Walk or cycle reasonable distances rather than taking the car.
- Walk round the block in your lunch hour.
- If you can't go out, try walking up and down stairs a few times a day.
- Re-introduce the traditional habit of a family walk after the Sunday roast.
- Get off the bus or tube one stop earlier than usual and walk the rest of the way.
- Start getting up an hour earlier than usual and go for a walk, cycle, do some gardening, fetch the daily paper, or visit the gym.
- Buy a home exercise machine and use it while watching the evening news.

Regular exercise also has other health benefits. It can help to postpone the effects of ageing and can even prolong your life—even if it is not started until middle age. A study of more than 10,000 men found that exercise reduced the number of age-related deaths from all causes by almost a quarter, even if exercise was not started until middle age. In particular, deaths from coronary heart disease (CHD) were reduced by

41 per cent, whether or not the men had other risk factors such as overweight, high blood pressure or smoking cigarettes. Exercise can also:

- reduce anxiety and tension;
- improve your quality of sleep;
- boost your creativity;
- lift your mood;
- help you maintain a healthy weight;
- reduce fat storage around your abdomen so that you become less apple-shaped;
- stimulate your bowels and help to keep them regular;
- reduce high blood cholesterol levels;
- reduce high blood pressure;
- reduce your risk of stroke by up to 50 per cent;
- reduce your risk of diabetes by up to 40 per cent;
- reduce your risk of intestinal haemorrhage;
- reduce your risk of cancer of the colon, rectum or womb by up to a quarter.

Unfortunately, seven out of ten men, and eight out of ten women, do not take enough exercise to reduce their risk of heart attack or to give significant protection against osteo-porosis.

Using your pulse rate
Measuring your pulse rate during exercise will ensure you stay within the safe levels for burning fat, getting fit and strengthen-ing your bones without overstressing your heart. Your pulse is most easily felt:

- on the inner side of your wrist, on the same side as your thumb (radial pulse);
- at the side of the neck, under the jaw (carotid pulse).

Count your pulse after sitting quietly for around 15 minutes. This is your resting pulse rate. The heart beats approximately

70 times per minute in the average fit person, although some medications (e.g. beta-blockers) are designed to slow your heart to around 60 beats per minute to reduce the workload of your heart. Assuming you are not taking any drugs, your resting pulse rate gives a rough assessment of your overall fitness level:

RESTING PULSE RATE (beats per minute)	LEVEL OF FITNESS
50–59	Excellent (trained athletes)
60–69	Good
70–79	Fair
80 or over	Poor

To ensure your heart is not being overstressed during exercise, take your pulse rate over ten seconds, and make sure it stays within the ten-second pulse range for your age, as shown on the following table:

AGE	TEN-SECOND PULSE RANGE
20–29	20–27
30–39	19–25
40–49	18–23
50–59	17–22
60–69	16–21
70	15–20

Take your ten-second pulse every ten minutes or so during your exercise period. If you are unfit, make sure your pulse stays at the lower end of your ten-second pulse range at first, and slowly work up to the upper end of the range over several weeks.

If at any time your pulse rate goes higher than it should,

stop exercising and walk around slowly until your pulse falls. When you restart, take things a little more easily.

Try taking your pulse one minute after stopping exercise, too. The more rapidly your pulse rate falls, the fitter you are. After ten minutes' rest, your heart rate should fall to below 100 beats per minute. If you are very fit, your pulse will drop by up to 70 beats in one minute.

- At the end of 20 minutes' exercise, you should feel invigorated rather than exhausted.
- Stop if at any time you develop pain, become so breathless you can't speak, develop chest tightness or pain, feel dizzy or unwell and seek medical advice if appropriate.

Varying your routine
It is worth changing your exercise routine regularly—perhaps every six months. Research shows that in women aged over 55 (i.e. post-menopausal) bone density peaks around six months after starting a regular exercise regime such as weight training or aerobics, but that this benefit is lost after a year. Therefore, if you continue to exercise in the same way, all you are doing is maintaining bone mass (which is better than not exercising, when bone mass would fall) rather than building new bone and increasing bone density. By changing the type of exercise you do, your bones will experience new stresses in different areas that continue the bone-building process for optimum effect.

Is too much exercise bad for you?
While regular exercise increases bone density and protects against osteoporosis, it is possible to go too far. Excessive exercise—especially if coupled with a calcium-poor diet—can lead to bone weakening and the development of stress fractures.

If a woman exercises so much that her periods stop, her

oestrogen levels will fall. This has a similar effect on the bones as lack of oestrogen after the menopause and her bone density will rapidly decrease by 2–3 per cent per year. By taking calcium supplements and reducing excessive levels of exercise down to recommended levels, however, menstruation will return and average bone mineral density will start to increase again.

Exercise should always be kept within sensible levels and professional sports persons should ideally train under professional supervision.

Stretch exercises to help your bones and joints

The following stretch exercises can also help to improve your joint mobility, strengthen your muscles and bones and reduce your risk of osteoporosis. Repeat them at least five to ten times, once or twice a day:

Neck stretch: Stand comfortably with feet apart and shoulders relaxed. Slowly drop your left ear towards your left shoulder and hold the stretch for a count of five. Repeat with the right ear.

Shoulders: Stand comfortably, with feet apart. Bend your arms up and clasp your hands behind your head. Pull your elbows forward so they almost touch in front of your chin, then swing your elbows out so they are as wide apart as possible.

Put your arms up behind your back as if trying to fasten your bra (or if you prefer, putting your hands in your back pockets) then lower then again.

Raise your arms above your head, keeping them straight, and stretch as high as you can.

Raise one arm out to your side and slowly swing it around to make a big circle.

Arms: Stand facing a wall, two feet away, with your feet a hip width apart. Keep your back straight, your abdominal muscles pulled in and your pelvis tilted forward. Place your hands flat on the wall, in line with your shoulders, with your fingers pointing up. Do 'push-ups' by bending your elbows and leaning in so your nose almost touches the wall—keep your back flat and legs straight. Hold this position briefly then use your arms to push away from the wall. (Breathe in as you bend in, breathe out as you push out.)

Wrists: Bend both wrists up and down, side to side and round and round as far as possible.

Fingers: Squeeze a soft foam ball in the palm of your hand by clenching your fingers as tightly as possible. Hold for a count of five, then relax and straighten your fingers.

Pelvis: Lie on the floor, or a firm mattress. Bend your knees up, and place your feet flat on the floor and relax your arms on the floor above your head. Now tighten the muscles of your lower abdomen and buttocks, so your pelvis tilts and the small of your back flattens against the floor. Hold for a count of five, then relax and repeat.

Hips: Stand comfortably with feet apart and hands on your hips. Without moving your lower body, rotate your upper body and hips to the right, to the back, to the left and to the front again. Repeat five times in one direction, then five times in the other.

Lie on the floor, with both legs bent so that your feet are flat on the floor. Lift one leg up into the air and straighten it. Hold for a count of five. Repeat with the other leg. (Note: when straightening one leg, always keep the other knee bent to protect your back. Don't try to lift both legs into the air at the same time.)

EXERCISES TO HELP STRENGTHEN YOUR BONES

Legs: Stand comfortably with your back and head straight, tummy tucked in and feet apart. Rest your left hand on a table for support. Bend your left knee slightly, and raise your right leg to grasp your right ankle with your right hand. Keep your knees facing forward. Gently ease your foot in towards your bottom until you feel a mild stretch. Hold for a count of five. Repeat with the other side.

Stand with your back two feet away from a wall, your feet a hip width apart and your toes pointing forwards. Pull in your abdominal muscles, relax your shoulders, and bend your knees and hips to around 90 degrees, pressing your lower back into the wall. Hold this position for at least 50 seconds.

Stand comfortably with feet apart, knees bent and hands on your knees. Flex your knees up and down, keeping them bent throughout. Don't let your bottom go lower than the level of your knees.

Ankles: Stand comfortably, resting one hand on a table for support. Lift one foot and rotate the ankle in ten complete circles, first clockwise, then anticlockwise. Repeat with the other foot.

Stand comfortably, feet slightly apart, with one hand resting on a table for support. Lift both heels up so that you are standing on the ball of your foot, then relax down again.

CHAPTER 4

Diet and Osteoporosis

As stressed at the beginning of this book, osteoporosis is largely a preventable disease. By making relatively simple changes to your diet you can go a long way to preventing brittle bones and future fractures. In fact, your diet has such a profound effect on bone health that it is never too late—or too early—to start eating for better bones.

There are several ways in which your diet and nutritional state affect your hormone balance and bone health. Most people are aware of the importance of a high calcium diet, but several other factors play a role too. The most important dietary links with your risk of osteoporosis are the amount of:

- natural plant hormones (phyto-oestrogens) present in your food;
- essential fatty acids you obtain;
- saturated fat you eat;
- fibre you eat;
- protein you eat;
- vitamins, minerals and trace elements you absorb.

NATURAL PLANT OESTROGENS

Many plants contain natural chemicals that have a weak, hormone-like action in the human body. These plant hormones, known as phyto-oestrogens and phytoprogesterones, can help to maintain falling hormone levels after the menopause and protect against osteoporosis, as well as improving menopausal symptoms such as hot flushes, night sweats, fatigue and low sex drive. Plants rich in oestrogen-like substances include:

Seeds: Almost all, especially linseeds, pumpkin seeds, sesame seeds, sunflower seeds and sprouted seeds (e.g. alfalfa, mung beans, lentils, red clover, soya beans).

Nuts: Almonds, cashew nuts, hazelnuts, peanuts, walnuts and nut oils.

Wholegrains: Almost all, especially corn, buckwheat, millet, oats, rye, wheat.

Fresh fruits: Apples, avocados, bananas, mangoes, papayas, rhubarb.

Dried fruits: Especially dates, figs, prunes, raisins, which are all high in calcium, too.

Vegetables: Dark green leafy vegetables (e.g. broccoli, pak choi, spinach) and exotic members of the cruciferous family (e.g. Chinese leaves, kohlrabi); celery, fennel.

Legumes: Especially soya beans and soya products (e.g. tofu, tempeh, miso, tamari), lentils.

Cooking herbs: Especially angelica, chervil, chives, garlic, ginger, horseradish, nutmeg, parsley, rosemary, sage, seaweed (kelp, Irish moss), nettles and watercress.

Honey: Especially that made from wild flowers, also bee pollen and royal jelly supplements.

For further information on oestrogenic herbal supplements, see chapter 7.

Plant hormones damp down menopausal symptoms and protect against osteoporosis. At the same time, they seem to protect against two common Western diseases—cancer of the breast in women and cancer of the prostate gland in men.

The traditional Japanese diet is low in fat, especially saturated fat, and consists of rice, soya products (e.g. soya beans, soya meal, tofu) and fish together with legumes, grains and yellow-green vegetables such as cruciferous plants—these include exotic members of the cabbage and turnip families (e.g. kohlrabi, Chinese leaves). Soya and cruciferous plants are rich sources of isoflavonoids—weak plant oestrogens (phyto-oestrogens) that are converted into hormone-like substances by bacteria fermentation in the gut and then absorbed into the circulation. As a result, the Japanese have blood levels of these phyto-oestrogens that are up to 110 times higher than in the Western world. This is not a genetic effect, for when Japanese people move to the West and follow a typical Western diet, their blood hormone levels and risk of illnesses such as coronary heart disease and cancer quickly become similar to those of the local population.

Plant oestrogens are sufficiently similar to our own human oestrogens to trigger production of a protein, sex hormone binding globulin (SHBG). This mops up the dietary oestrogens and carries them round the body to where they are needed, including your arteries and bones. Plant hormones help to reduce menopausal symptoms to the extent that Japanese women do not have an equivalent word or phrase meaning 'hot flush'. Phyto-oestrogens also mimic the natural oestrogen effect on arteries—which may help to explain why the Japanese have one of the lowest rates of coronary heart disease in the world. Plant hormones may also protect against osteoporosis.

Increasing your intake of fruit and vegetables, which contain plant hormones as well as vitamins and minerals including potassium bicarbonate (see p.164), has been shown to decrease the risk of osteoporosis. Aim to eat at least five servings of fruit, vegetables or salad per day (not counting potatoes). This may seem like a lot but is fairly easy to do—for example, the following adds up to a total of seven servings:

—fresh orange juice with breakfast;
—banana mid-morning;
—large salad and an apple with lunch;
—two servings of vegetables (e.g. spinach, carrots) with dinner;
—fresh fruit for dessert.

An Australian bread fortified with soya and linseed to make it rich in natural plant oestrogens is now also available in the UK. Eating at least four slices of Burgen bread per day will help to damp down hot flushes and night sweats and to reduce the risk of osteoporosis. Eat Burgen bread for its delicious nutty flavour—and consider any health benefits a bonus. Burgen bread is produced in the UK by Allied Bakeries and should be available in all main supermarkets.

ESSENTIAL FATTY ACIDS

A diet rich in certain essential fatty acids (EFAs) seems to stimulate calcium uptake from the gut, decrease calcium loss in the urine and trigger increased calcium deposition in bone. Increasing your intake of essential fatty acids, as well as boosting your calcium intake, will help to protect against osteoporosis.

Essential fatty acids (EFAs) cannot be made in large quantities in the body and must therefore come from your food. There are two main EFAs:

- linoleic acid (an omega-6 polyunsaturated fatty acid);
- linolenic acid (an omega-3 polyunsaturated fatty acid).

Once in your body, these two EFAs act as building blocks to make cell membranes, nerve linings, sex hormones (including oestrogen) and hormone-like chemicals known as prostaglandins.

As a result of following low-fat diets for general health, lack of essential fatty acids is common. At least eight out of ten people are thought to be deficient in EFAs, and unless you are eating the equivalent of 30g (1¼oz) of nuts or seeds per day, your diet is likely to be poor in them.

The way you handle EFAs can also be blocked by a variety of diet and lifestyle factors which can contribute to deficiency, including:

- eating too much saturated (animal) fat;
- eating too much trans-fatty acid (e.g. found in some margarines);
- eating too much sugar;
- drinking too much alcohol;
- deficiency of vitamins and minerals, especially vitamin B6, zinc and magnesium;
- crash-dieting;
- smoking cigarettes;
- exposure to pollution;
- being under excessive stress.

If your diet is lacking in EFAs, your metabolism can make do with the next best fatty acids available (e.g. those derived from saturated fats), but this is not ideal. Every cell in your body is surrounded by a fatty envelope known as the cell membrane. When your diet is rich in EFAs, your cell membranes (including those in bone cells) contain a higher percentage of these and are flexible, healthy and youthful. If your diet is poor in EFAs, your cell membranes include more of other types of fat that tend to make them more rigid and more prone to dryness, itching and premature ageing. Your cell membranes also contain receptors that interact with circulating hormones such as oestrogen, and if you lack EFAs your hormones cannot interact with your tissues—including bone—as well as they should.

As EFAs also act as building blocks for sex hormones, lack of them leads to hormone and prostaglandin imbalances. These imbalances can increase your risk of developing inflammatory diseases (e.g. acne, asthma, psoriasis, rheumatoid arthritis), blood clots, cyclical breast pain, irregular periods, menopausal symptoms, dry itchy skin and osteoporosis. Lack of EFAs also affects the function of vitamin D so that less calcium is absorbed from the gut and deposited in your bones.

The EFAs that are of most benefit for bone health are gammalinolenic acid (GLA—found in evening primrose and starflower oils) and eicosapentaenoic acid (EPA—found in oily fish). To boost your intake of EFAs, try eating more:

- nuts and seeds—try sprinkling them onto cereals, yoghurt, desserts and salads;
- bread enriched with soya beans and linseed (e.g. Burgen bread);
- green vegetables, especially the dark green leafy ones;
- oily fish such as mackerel, herring, salmon, trout, sardines and pilchards (tuna is not classed as oily but still contains beneficial oils)—aim for at least 300g per week;
- sunflower, olive and rapeseed oils in cooking and salad dressings;
- evening primrose oil as a supplement (500mg for general preventative health, up to 3g per day to treat a particular condition such as cyclical breast pain);
- linoleic acid alone is found in sunflower seed, almonds, corn, sesame seed, safflower oil and extra virgin olive oil;
- linolenic acid alone is found in evening primrose oil, starflower (borage) seed oil and blackcurrant seed oils which are available as food supplements;
- both linoleic and linolenic acids are found in rich quantities in walnuts, pumpkin seeds, soya beans, linseed oil, rapeseed oil and flax oil.

When taking an EFA supplement, you will soon start to notice a beneficial effect on your nails, which become thicker, stronger and less prone to splitting. This is a good indication that your bones are becoming stronger, too.

The action of essential fatty acids is boosted by vitamin E which helps to preserve it in the body. If you are taking an evening primrose oil supplement, either take one containing both GLA and vitamin E, or take vitamin E capsules at the same time (100–400iu).

Certain vitamins and minerals are also needed during the metabolism of essential fatty acids. These are vitamin C, vitamin B6, vitamin B3 (niacin), zinc and magnesium. If you are taking evening primrose oil, you should therefore ensure that your intake of these is adequate (e.g. by taking a multinutrient supplement, see chapter 5).

The only people who should not take evening primrose oil are those who are allergic to it and those with a relatively rare nervous disorder known as temporal lobe epilepsy.

SATURATED FATS

A high intake of saturated fat reduces absorption of two important bone minerals from the gut—calcium and magnesium. As a result, a high fat diet is linked with loss of calcium from the body and an increased risk of osteoporotic fractures.

A low fat diet is equally harmful to health, so don't go too low as dietary fats are important to supply:

- energy;
- essential fatty acids;
- fat-soluble vitamins A, D and E;
- building blocks for cell membranes, nerve linings, hormones and bile salts.

Fat intakes in the Western world average over 40 per cent of daily calorie intake, of which over 15 per cent is saturated (mainly animal) fat. Ideally, fat intake needs to be cut back so it makes up no more than 30 per cent of your daily calories, with saturated fats supplying no more than 10 per cent of daily energy intake. This is best done by eating a wider variety of foods, including more pasta, bread, rice and boiled or baked potatoes.

- Avoid obviously fatty foods.
- Buy lean cuts of meat and trim off visible fat.
- Have several vegetarian meals per week, which include pulses and beans for protein.
- Switch to reduced-fat versions of mayonnaise, salad dress-

ing, cheese, milk, yoghurt, etc., rather than full-fat ones.

- Eat baked potatoes rather than roasted or chipped.
- Grill food rather than frying to help fat drain away.
- Soak up excess fat from cooked foods using kitchen roll.
- Cut down on cakes, doughnuts, chips, biscuits, pastries and crisps.

FIBRE

Dietary fibre—or roughage—is the indigestible part of plant foods that cannot be broken down in the human gut. Although roughage provides little in the way of energy or nutrients, it is essential for helping the digestion and absorption of other foods. Fibre encourages the muscular, wave-like bowel movements that push digested food through your system. A high-fibre diet helps to prevent constipation, diverticular disease, irritable bowel syndrome and some bowel tumours. The main sources of dietary fibre are:

- unrefined complex carbohydrates such as wholemeal bread, wholegrain cereals, wholewheat pasta and brown rice;
- nuts, seeds and pulses;
- root vegetables and fresh or dried fruits;
- breakfast cereals containing bran.

Eating too much fibre can actually make menopausal symptoms worse and possibly increase the risk of osteoporosis. A large percentage of hormones in the bloodstream are taken up by the liver, secreted into the bile and then into the gut. These are then reabsorbed from the gut. This is known as the entero-hepatic circulation of hormones. If you eat too much fibre, this can bind some of the oestrogen in the gut so that it is more likely to be cleared from the body than reabsorbed. Unless you have problems with constipation, it is a good idea not to take fibre supplements on a long-term basis, but to increase the amount of fruit and vegetables (which are also rich in plant hormones) instead. Recommended levels of fibre intake are around 30g (1¼oz) per day. Average intakes of fibre are low, however, at around 20g (¾oz) per day, so excess fibre is rarely a significant risk for osteoporosis.

Bran-containing breakfast cereals provide one of the highest concentrations of dietary fibre. The list below gives the fibre content per 100g (4oz) of some high-fibre foods. Fractions of ounces are approximate equivalents:

Bran	40g (1½oz)
Dried apricots	18g (½oz)
Peas	5g (¼oz)
Prunes	13g (½oz)
Cooked brown rice	4g (¼oz)
Cooked wholemeal spaghetti	4g (¼oz)
Brown bread	6g (¼oz)
Walnuts	6g (¼oz)

PROTEIN

Protein makes up around a third of the weight of your bones as it forms the framework on which calcium and other salts are deposited. Both a low protein intake and an excessively high protein intake will increase your risk of osteoporosis. Low protein intakes are rare in the Western world. The recommended intake for adults is around 40–55g (1½–2¼oz) depending on age and sex. Most adults obtain more than this— intakes of 80g–90g (3¼–3½oz) are common. Dietary protein can be divided into two groups:

- First class proteins—contain significant quantities of the essential amino acids, for example animal meat, fish, eggs, dairy products.
- Second class proteins—contain some essential amino acids but not all, for example vegetables, rice, beans, nuts.

Second class proteins need to be mixed and matched by eating as wide a variety of foods as possible—for example, the essential amino acid missing from haricot beans is found in bread. Hence, combining cereals with pulses or seeds and nuts provides a balanced amino acid intake. People who do not eat meat can obtain a balanced protein intake by eating a combination of five parts rice to one part beans. It is unlikely that vegetarians (with the exception of fruitarians) will be deficient in protein.

If you feel your protein intake is low for any reason, and you want to increase it, it is best to eat more fish, white meat, wholegrains, nuts, seeds and beans rather than increasing your intake of red meat and full-fat dairy products which (apart from egg white) are also high in saturated fat. One study, for example, found that women who had followed a lactovegetarian diet (avoiding meat, fish and eggs but eating dairy products such as milk) for at least 20 years had lost only 18 per cent of their bone mineral by the age of 80, compared with 35 per cent less bone in meat-eaters. It may seem surprising that vegetarians can get enough protein from their diet, until you consider that large-boned mammals such as elephants are in fact herbivores (plant eaters).

Even people who eat meat or fish daily get half their daily protein from non-meat sources. The average percentage of daily protein provided by various food groups is as follows:

meat products	36 per cent
cereal products	23 per cent
(mainly bread and pasta)	
milk and milk products	10 per cent
fruit and vegetables	10 per cent
fish	6 per cent
eggs	4 per cent

When protein is metabolised, acids are produced which must be buffered with calcium to make them harmless and to excrete them from the body. If you eat excess protein (more than 170g (5½oz) per day) and have a low calcium diet, calcium will be reabsorbed from your bones for this function. Eating too much protein is therefore harmful to bones. Cut back on meat intake (e.g. to no more than an average of 100g (4oz) per day) and eat more vegetable sources of protein instead. Surprisingly, one raw rump steak weighing 100g (4oz) provides only 19g (approx. ¾oz) of protein.

If your diet is high in meat protein, however, you can help to protect your bones by ensuring that you also eat plenty of calcium (at least 1500mg per day).

SALT

Many people are aware that the amount of table salt (sodium chloride) they eat is linked to their risk of high blood pressure or stroke in later life. Few realise that it also increases their risk of osteoporosis. A high sodium intake increases the loss of calcium through the kidneys into the urine. You can therefore help to prevent osteoporosis just by cutting back on your salt intake. Research suggests that halving average salt intake could cut calcium loss in the urine by as much as 20 per cent. This will also have other beneficial effects on health by reducing high blood pressure and reducing your risk of a heart attack or stroke.

Ideally, you should obtain no more than 4g–6g (¼oz) salt (sodium chloride) per day from your diet. Most people obtain at least 9g (⅜oz) of salt per day which is considered too high. Unfortunately, most dietary salt (around 75 per cent) is in the form of hidden salt, added to processed foods including canned products, ready-prepared meals, biscuits, cakes and breakfast cereals. Always check labels of bought products and do not eat those with a high content of sodium chloride. In particular, try to avoid:

- adding salt to food during cooking or at the table;
- obviously salty food such as salted nuts, crisps, bacon;
- tinned products, especially those canned in brine;
- cured, smoked or pickled fish/meats, meat pastes, pâtés;
- ready prepared meals;
- packet soups, sauces, stock cubes and yeast extracts.

Cut down on salt gradually and obtain flavour from spices, black pepper and herbs instead—that way, you won't miss it. Herbs are also an important source of vitamins, minerals (especially calcium) and antioxidants and most people would benefit from eating more of them.

Low potassium intake

Dietary potassium helps to flush excess sodium from the body through the kidneys. A diet that is low in potassium can increase your risk of osteoporosis—especially if your diet is also high in sodium. To increase your potassium intake eat more:

- seafood;
- fresh fruit, especially bananas, dried apricots, pears and tomatoes;
- fruit juices and fruit yoghurts;
- vegtetables especially mushrooms, potatoes, aubergines, peppers, squashes and spinach;
- pulses such as peas and lima beans;
- wholegrain breakfast cereals (check labels for sodium chloride content).

Low-salt products containing potassium chloride to replace sodium chloride are popular but can taste bitter. Steam rather than boil vegetables to retain more of their mineral content— or if you do cook them in water, make gravy or a low-fat sauce with it afterwards.

SUGAR

Most people eat too much sugar, which is linked with a range of long-term health problems including osteoporosis. A high sugar intake increases the loss of the minerals calcium, chromium, copper, magnesium and zinc from the body. It is therefore important to limit dietary sugars when taking steps to help prevent osteoporosis.

CAFFEINE

Caffeine has several effects in the body which may be harmful to bone. It increases loss of calcium and magnesium in the urine and also increases the amount of calcium absorbed from bone by both lowering blood calcium levels and increasing production of parathyroid hormone. Just two large cups of filter coffee (containing 300mg caffeine) can cause an extra 15mg calcium to be lost from the body. This may seem little, but if you have a high, regular intake of caffeine—especially after the menopause—it may contribute to as much as a 10 per cent fall in bone mass over a ten-year period. Some research suggests that women who drink four cups of coffee per day are three times more likely to suffer a hip fracture at some stage in their life. One recent study has suggested that women should obtain an extra 40g (1½oz) calcium for every 178ml (6fl oz) serving of caffeine-containing coffee consumed. You can help to prevent osteoporosis by avoiding excess caffeine intake, switching to decaffeinated brands of tea, coffee, cola, etc., as well as boosting your calcium intake to compensate for the amount of caffeine you do consume.

PHOSPHORUS

Phosphorus and calcium together form a salt, calcium phosphate, which is a major component of the minerals found in bone. In an ideal world, our diet should provide similar quantities of calcium and phosphorus. We commonly eat two to four times more phosphorus than calcium, however, as it is commonly added to foods during processing. Phosphated distarch phosphate, for example, is used as a stabiliser, thickening agent and binder, while phosphoric acid is used as an acidulant and flavouring agent (especially in fizzy drinks such as colas).

If excess phosphorus is absorbed from the diet into the circulation, it increases resorption of calcium from bone to balance it (by raising parathyroid hormone levels). Phosphates can also bind to magnesium and reduce the amount available in the body.

You can help to prevent osteoporosis by avoiding processed foods as much as possible, cutting back on your intake of meat, and checking labels so that you limit your intake of foods rich in phosphates and phosphoric acid.

WATER

Fluid is just as essential for good health as what you eat. Aim to drink at least three litres of fluid per day—preferably as mineral water, milk and fresh juice. Mineral water is a useful source of bone minerals such as calcium and magnesium, especially in hard water areas.

Summary: Dietary changes to help protect against osteoporosis

- Eat at least five portions of fresh fruit and vegetables per day.
- Eat more plants rich in plant hormones such as soya bean products, celéry, fennel, rhubarb and green and yellow vegetables—especially exotic members of the cabbage and turnip family such as Chinese leaves or kohlrabi.
- Eat more pulses such as chickpeas, lentils, broad beans, runner beans, etc.

- Eat more nuts, seeds, dark green leafy vegetables and oily fish for essential fatty acids.
- Consider taking supplements containing evening primrose and omega-3 fish oils.
- Eat more wholegrain cereals for essential fatty acids.
- Limit your overall intake of fat, especially saturated and trans-fatty acids.
- Avoid excess fibre intake (i.e. fibre supplements).
- Avoid too little or too much dietary protein—limit meat intake to around 100g (4oz) per day.
- Avoid or limit your intake of salt.
- Ensure you have a good intake of potassium.
- Avoid or limit your intake of sugar.
- Avoid or limit your intake of tea, coffee and other caffeinated drinks.
- Avoid or limit your intake of phosphoric acid and phosphates.
- Avoid convenience, pre-processed foods and additives—eat home-made meals as much as possible.
- Drink plenty of fluids, especially mineral or filtered water.

CHAPTER 5

Vitamins and Minerals for Bone Health

Certain vitamins and minerals are known to be essential for optimum bone health and the prevention of osteoporosis. These are:

MICRONUTRIENT	RECOMMENDED DAILY AMOUNT (EC RDA)
Boron	—
Calcium	800mg
Copper	—
Fluoride	—
Magnesium	300mg
Manganese	—
Phosporus	800mg
Silica	—
Strontium	—
Zinc	15mg
Vitamin A	800mcg
Vitamin B6 (pyridoxine)	2mg
Vitamin B12 (cyanocobalamin)	1mcg
Folic acid	200mcg
Vitamin C	60mg
Vitamin D	5mcg
Vitamin K	—

— No RDA yet established

This chapter looks at each of these vitamins and minerals in turn, showing why they are important for bone health, how much you need, and which foods normally supply them.

MINERALS

Minerals are inorganic elements, some of which are metals, that are essential for the smooth functioning of the metabolism. Those needed in amounts of less than 100mg per day are often referred to as trace elements. Minerals and trace elements can only come from your diet and depend on the quality of soil on which produce is grown or grazed.

The average adult contains around 3kg of minerals and trace elements, most of which are found in your bones.

Boron

Boron is a trace element that was only recently recognised as important for bone health, especially in post-menopausal women. It is found mainly in fruit and vegetables, and a high boron intake (around 10mg per day) may account for the lower risk of osteoporosis in vegetarians. Boron helps to normalise oestrogen production in post-menopausal women and boosts production of the active form of vitamin D.

EC RDA: None yet set. 3mg a day or more suggested for bone health.

Average daily intake: 0.5–1mg.

Research: A group of post-menopausal women followed a normal, low-boron diet for 17 weeks and were given boron supplements (3mg daily in the form of sodium borate capsules) for seven weeks. After just eight days' treatment, they excreted 44 per cent less calcium and 33 per cent less magnesium. They were also found to have almost doubled their production of both oestrogen and testosterone hormones. This suggests that boron can prevent calcium loss and bone demineralisation in post-menopausal women.

Possible signs of deficiency: Osteoporosis.

Good dietary sources: Fruits and vegetables, especially apples, grapes, pears, plums, prunes, strawberries, avocado, broccoli—eating the recommended five servings a day will provide 1.5–3mg boron.

Calcium

Calcium is the major structural mineral in bone, where it is present as calcium phosphate, also known as hydroxyapatite. Calcium is absorbed in the gut, a process that is dependent upon the presence of vitamin D. Usually, only 30–40 per cent of the calcium present in food and drinks is absorbed—the rest is lost in the bowel motions. Some types of fibre (phytates from wheat in unleavened bread such as chapatti) decrease calcium absorption by binding to calcium in the bowel and forming an insoluble, non-absorbable salt. High-fibre diets, which speed the passage of food through the bowels, also reduce calcium absorption.

Ninety-nine per cent of calcium absorbed from the gut goes straight into the bones and teeth. The other 1 per cent plays a crucial role in blood clotting, muscle contraction, nerve conduction, immune defences and the production of energy. A dietary deficiency at any stage in life means that bone stores of calcium are raided, significantly increasing the risk of future osteoporosis. Good intakes of calcium are therefore vital throughout life—during childhood and adolescence when bones are still developing, as well as in later years when bones are naturally starting to thin down.

EC RDA: 800mg.

The National Osteoporosis Society in the UK recommends higher daily intakes of calcium:

children 7–10 years	800mg per day
teenagers 11–18 years	1000mg per day
women 19–45 years	1000mg per day
women over 45 years	1500mg per day
men 19–60 years	1000mg per day
men over 60 years	1500mg per day
pregnancy	1200mg per day
breast-feeding	1250mg per day

Average daily intake: 820mg per day (NB: 50 per cent of people get less than this).

Research: Adding calcium supplements to the diet of elderly people reduces their risk of a vertebral fracture by 20 per cent, while giving them both calcium and vitamin D supplements may reduce their risk of non-vertebral and hip fracture by 30–40 per cent.

Possible signs of deficiency:

muscle aches and pains	infected gums (periodontal
muscle twitching and spasm	disease)
muscle cramps	loose teeth
tetany (sustained cramps)	convulsions
palpitations	dementia
receding gums	

Good dietary sources: Milk, yoghurt, cheese, green vegetables, oranges and bread. Small amounts of calcium also come from vegetables and hard water.

Calcium content of some foods

FOOD	CALCIUM CONTENT
Skimmed milk (600ml) (1 pint)	720mg per pint
Semi-skimmed milk (600ml) (1 pint)	720mg per pint
Whole milk (600ml) (1 pint)	690mg per pint
Soya milk (600ml) (1 pint)	78mg per pint
Whole milk yoghurt (150ml) (5fl oz)	300mg
Low fat yoghurt (150ml) (5fl oz)	285mg
Parmesan cheese (30g) (1¼oz)	360mg
Cheddar cheese (30g) (1¼oz)	216mg
Feta cheese (30g) (1¼oz)	108mg
Fromage frais (30g) (1¼oz)	27mg
Cottage cheese (30g) (1¼oz)	22mg
2 slices white bread	76mg
2 slices brown bread	76mg
2 slices wholemeal bread	41mg
1 egg	25mg
1 large orange	58mg
Kelp (seaweed) (100g) (4oz)	1093mg
Sardines, canned (100g) (4oz)	540mg
Spinach, boiled (100g) (4oz)	170mg
Chickpeas, dried (100g) (4oz)	160mg
Brazil nuts (56g) (2¼oz)	101mg
Figs, dried (28g) (1oz)	78mg
Baked beans (112g) (4½oz)	50mg
Winter cabbage, boiled (112g) (4½oz)	43mg

See also calcium tables in appendices.

It is relatively easy to increase your intake of calcium. The simplest way is to drink an extra pint of skimmed or semi-skimmed milk per day. This provides as much calcium as whole milk but without the additional fat. Spinach and other dark green leafy vegetables are also excellent sources.

By law in the UK, white and brown flour must be fortified with calcium—but this does not apply to wholemeal flour. So, if your calcium intake is likely to be low (e.g. if you don't like milk or milk products), brown bread is the better choice.

Ideally, as much calcium as possible should come from simple adjustments to your diet. If you are unable to eat dairy products, however, calcium supplements are important. Some supplements contain calcium salts which are relatively insoluble and pass through the gut unabsorbed. The salts that are best absorbed are calcium lactate (the form found in milk), calcium gluconate and calcium citrate.

Test your supplement by adding it to vinegar at room temperature and stirring every five minutes. If it hasn't dissolved after 30 minutes, it is unlikely to do so in your stomach either—switch to another brand. Effervescent tablets, those that dissolve in water to make citrus-flavoured or calcium-enriched drinks (e.g. Calcium Clear), are the most useful type of calcium supplement.

Calcium tablets are best taken with meals. Some evidence suggests they are better taken with your evening meal rather than breakfast as calcium flux is greatest in the body at night, when growth hormone is secreted.

Taking calcium supplements together with essential fatty acid supplements (such as evening primrose or fish oils) will help to boost absorption and deposition of calcium into your bones. People with a tendency to kidney stones should only take calcium supplements together with essential fatty acids.

Copper

Copper is a trace element that is needed in small amounts for many metabolic reactions. It is essential for the production of brain chemicals, skin pigment (melanin) and the red blood pigment haemoglobin, as well as for healthy bones. Copper is essential for the synthesis of collagen, the structural protein that forms the matrix on which calcium salts are laid down to form your bone structure. It is therefore involved in maintaining healthy bones, cartilage, hair and skin—especially their elasticity.

EC RDA: None yet set. Intakes between 0.8–1.2mg are suggested.

Average daily intake: 1.6mg/day (NB: 50 per cent of people get less than this and copper deficiency is common).

Research: Copper-deficient diets have been shown to reduce bone mineralisation and bone strength. Many people with arthritis have low blood levels of copper, and are helped by wearing a copper bracelet so that trace amounts are absorbed through the skin.

Possible signs of deficiency:
anaemia
low white blood cell count and increased susceptibility to
    infection
fluid retention
loss of taste sensation
raised blood cholesterol levels
abnormal structure and pigmentation of body hair
abnormal pigmentation and loss of elasticity in skin
irritability
osteoporosis

Good dietary sources: Crustaceans (e.g. prawns), shellfish (e.g. oysters), brewer's yeast, olives, nuts, pulses, wholegrain cereals, green vegetables grown in copper-rich soil.

Up to 70 per cent of dietary intake remains unabsorbed because it is bound to other bowel contents such as sugar, sweeteners, refined flour, raw meat, vitamin C, zinc and calcium. Copper supplementation may therefore be important in preventing osteoporosis if the diet is deficient. The ideal dietary ratio of copper to zinc is 1:10.

Fluoride

Fluoride is a mineral important for healthy bones and teeth. It is well known for binding to tooth enamel and strengthening it to help prevent decay. In the same way, small amounts of fluoride can bind to bone to produce calcium fluorapatite which is more resistant to reabsorption. Excess fluoride can cause formation of abnormal, weakened bone, however, and cause discoloured teeth (fluorosis). Fluorosis seems to triple the risk of osteoporotic fractures and may also increase the risk of bone cancer.

EC RDA: None set. Intakes of 1.5–4mg have been suggested as desirable. Fluoridation of drinking water supplies 1–3mg fluoride per day.

Average daily intake: 1.82mg (2.9mg in areas with fluoridated water).

Possible signs of deficiency: Dental caries, osteoporosis.

Good dietary sources:

tea leaves provide 70 per cent of dietary fluoride	eggs
	lettuce
fluoridated water supplies	cabbage
seafood, especially oysters	lentils
milk	wholegrains

Fluoride supplements are not recommended, but people who drink large amounts of tea may gain some benefit in the long-term prevention of osteoporosis.

Magnesium

Magnesium is an important mineral, with 70 per cent of body stores found in the bones and teeth. It is essential for maintaining salt balance across cell membranes, for the transmission of electrical messages across cells and for generating the heart-beat. Few enzymes can work without it and magnesium is now known to be vital for healthy tissues, including bones. Magnesium regulates production of calcitonin and parathyroid hormone, both of which are involved in bone remodelling. Magnesium is also needed to activate vitamin D so that calcium can be absorbed from the gut, and for the production of bone crystals by the enzyme alkaline phosphatase.

EC RDA: 300mg.

Average daily intake: 320mg (NB: 50 per cent of people get less than this and magnesium deficiency is widespread).

Research: Even a mild magnesium deficiency can lead to osteoporosis, and magnesium levels in red blood cells are lower in women with osteoporosis than those without. Taking magnesium supplements (250–750mg daily) for two years has been shown to increase bone mineral density by 1–8 per cent. One recent study found that women who took magnesium supplements instead of calcium for eight months increased their bone density by 11 per cent compared with those not taking magnesium. However, because of the interaction between magnesium and calcium, it is best to take both.

Possible signs of deficiency:

loss of appetite	change in bowel habit
nausea	confusion
fatigue	nervousness
muscle weakness, trembling and cramps	insomnia
	palpitations
numbness and tingling	dizziness
loss of co-ordination	osteoporosis
pre-menstrual syndrome	

Good dietary sources:

soya beans	milk and dairy products
nuts	wholegrains
brewer's yeast	bananas
brown rice	dark green leafy vegetables
seafood	chocolate
meat	drinking water in hard-water
eggs	areas

See also magnesium tables in appendices.

Magnesium and calcium work closely together and if you are taking supplements of one, you should also take the other, preferably in a ratio of two calcium to one magnesium. Processing removes most magnesium from foods.

Manganese

Manganese is an essential mineral, found in bones and soft tissues, which is important for normal structure, growth and development. It is involved in many metabolic functions, including the synthesis of amino acids, carbohydrates, sex hormones, blood clotting factors, cholesterol and some brain transmitters. It also acts as an antioxidant. Manganese is essential for production of cartilage, collagen and structural molecules known as mucopolysaccharides, all of which are important for the formation, repair, mineralisation and remodelling of bone.

EC RDA: None set. Intakes of 2–5mg per day are suggested.

Average daily intake: 4.6mg (tea drinkers), 2.3mg daily (non-tea drinkers).

Research: Women with osteoporosis have been found to have manganese levels that were four times lower than those without osteoporosis. Some researchers suggest that up to 7mg manganese are needed daily for optimum bone health.

Possible signs of deficiency:

reddening of body hair	poor blood clotting
scaly skin	glucose intolerance
poor growth of hair and nails	poor memory
disc and cartilage problems	osteoporosis

Good dietary sources:

black tea (one cup of tea contains 1mg manganese)	egg
	green leafy vegetables/herbs
wholegrains	offal
nuts and seeds	shellfish
fruits	milk

Processing removes much of the manganese content of wholegrain foods.

Phosphorus

The body contains between 500–800g of phosphorus, of which 90 per cent is found in the bones and teeth. It combines with calcium to form a salt, calcium phosphate, also known as hydroxyapatite. Phosphorus forms energy-rich chemicals that drive metabolic reactions and activate the vitamin B complex. Vitamin D is essential for absorption of phosphorus (and calcium) from the gut and for its deposition in bones. A balance between calcium and phosphorus is essential for bone health and both too much and too little phosphorus can lead to osteoporosis (see p.55). It is important to avoid high-phosphorus drinks such as colas when trying to prevent osteoporosis.

EC RDA: 800mg per day.

Average daily intake: 1200–1500mg.

Possible signs of deficiency: Deficiency is unusual, but can develop with long-term use of antacids containing aluminium hydroxide which impairs absorption of phosphates from the gut.

general malaise	numbness
loss of appetite	pins and needles
increased susceptibility to infection	irritability
	confusion
anaemia due to shortened life of red blood cells	joint stiffness
	bone pain
muscle weakness and tremor	osteomalacia/osteoporosis

Good dietary sources: Milk and milk products, yeast extract, soya beans, nuts, wholegrain cereals, eggs, poultry, meat and fish.

Silicon
Although silicon in its pure form is biologically inactive, it is now recognised as an essential trace element. In its soluble (colloidal) state, silicic acid, it is essential to human health—if intakes are deficient, normal growth cannot occur. The highest concentration of silica (silicon oxide) is found in connective tissues, cartilage and skin where it strengthens collagen and elastin fibres and contributes to tissue elasticity. The silica acid content of skin and bones decreases with age as tissues become increasingly inelastic and brittle.

EC RDA: None set. Intakes of 20–30mg daily have been suggested.

Average daily intake: 29mg.

Research: Supplements containing silica strengthen bone by cross-linking collagen strands. Silica has been shown to increase mineralisation in growing bones, especially in people whose calcium intakes are low. It is also needed for the formation of cartilage.

Possible signs of deficiency: Premature skin ageing, brittle hair and nails, hardening of the arteries, abnormal bone formation, osteoporosis.

Good dietary sources:

rice bran	green leafy vegetables
wholegrain wheat	potatoes
unprocessed barley, oats, rye,	sweet peppers
the herb horsetail (*Equisetum*	parsnips
arvense).	nuts and seeds

Strontium

Strontium is a mineral that is closely related to calcium and behaves in a similar way to calcium in the body, so that 99 per cent of our strontium stores (around 320mg) are found in bones and teeth. The amount of strontium in biological tissues is usually around one thousandth of the concentration of calcium. Strontium seems to strengthen teeth—and therefore presumably bone—as people living in areas where the strontium content of drinking water is high have fewer dental caries. Excess may damage teeth, however, as with fluoride.

Stable strontium, which is non-toxic, is often confused with radioactive strontium-90, produced in radioactive fallout from atomic bombs. This is long-lived and hazardous when incorporated into bone. Stable strontium may help to replace strontium-90 in bones and therefore help with detoxification.

EC RDA: None set. Intakes of 3mg–1g per day have been suggested.

Average daily intake: 1mg.

Research: One study suggests that strontium may be beneficial in the treatment of established osteoporosis. Six volunteers were given supplements of strontium (600–700mg per day) for six months. Biopsies showed this increased bone formation by over 170 per cent as well as reducing bone pain. Response was better in younger patients.

Possible signs of deficiency: Dental caries, osteoporosis.

Good dietary sources: Milk and dairy products, brazil nuts, bran, root vegetable peel.

Zinc

Zinc is essential for the proper function of more than a hundred different enzymes. It helps to regulate protein synthesis in response to hormone triggers and is vital for growth, sexual maturity, healing and immunity. Zinc enhances the actions of vitamin D and is essential for calcium absorption, production of bone collagen and for bone repair.

EC RDA: 15mg.

Average daily intake: Men 11mg, women 8mg (NB: 50 per cent of people get less than this and deficiency is widespread, especially in males as each ejaculate contains around 5mg zinc—one third of the daily requirement).

Research: Women with osteoporosis have been found to have blood and bone levels of zinc that are up to 30 per cent lower than in women with healthy bones.

Possible signs of deficiency:

poor growth and delayed puberty
impaired fertility
post-natal depression
poor wound healing
skin problems such as eczema, psoriasis, acne
poor hair and nail growth
white spots on nails
impaired immunity and increased risk of infection
loss of taste and smell sensations
poor appetite
diarrhoea
visual disturbances
mental slowing
sleep disturbances
osteoporosis

One of the earliest symptoms of zinc deficiency is loss of taste sensation. This can be tested for by obtaining a solution of zinc sulphate (5mg/5ml) from a chemist (e.g. Lambert's DuoZinc). Swirl a teaspoonful in your mouth. If the solution seems tasteless, zinc deficiency is likely. If the solution tastes furry, of minerals or slightly sweet, zinc levels are borderline. If it tastes strongly unpleasant, zinc levels are normal.

Good dietary sources: Red meat, seafood, especially oysters, offal, brewer's yeast, whole grains, pulses, eggs, cheese (see also zinc tables in appendices).

Food processing removes most mineral zinc from foods.

VITAMINS

Vitamins are naturally-occurring, organic substances which, although they are only needed in minute amounts, are essential for life. They cannot be synthesised in the body, or are only made in tiny amounts (e.g. vitamin D, niacin) which are too small to meet your needs. They must therefore come from your food.

Most vitamins act as essential intermediaries or catalysts to keep metabolic reactions running smoothly and efficiently. They are classified into two main groups:

71

- the fat-soluble vitamins (A, D, E and K) which dissolve in fat and are stored in the body—mainly in the liver;
- the water-soluble vitamins (B group and C) which dissolve in water and are easily lost in urine. These cannot be stored in the body in appreciable amounts (with the exception of vitamin B12) and must be continually replenished from the diet.

Vitamin A

Dietary vitamin A occurs in two main forms:

- preformed vitamin A (retinol), which is found only in animal foods;
- carotenoids (mainly beta-carotene) which are found only in plant sources.

Beta-carotene is made up of two molecules of vitamin A joined together, which can be split to yield vitamin A. Nutritionally, 6mcg beta-carotene is equivalent to around 1mcg of preformed retinol. Zinc is essential for this conversion. On average, around half of ingested beta-carotene is converted into vitamin A in the cells lining the small intestine and in the liver. As vitamin A is fat-soluble, it is stored in the liver and excess is harmful.

Vitamin A binds to special receptors inside cells and regulates the way genes are read to produce enzymes and other proteins. It helps to control growth and is essential for healthy skin, mucous membranes, teeth and bones, being involved in the development of bone-building cells (osteoblasts). Its role in preventing osteoporosis is not yet clear, however.

EC RDA: 800mcg.

Average daily intake: 926mcg (women)–1100mcg (men). NB: 50 per cent of people get less than this.

Possible signs of deficiency:
increased susceptibility to infection
scaly skin with raised, pimply hair follicles
flaking scalp
brittle, dull hair
poor eyesight and night vision
loss of appetite
dry, burning, itchy eyes
eye ulceration
inflamed gums and mucous membranes

Good dietary sources:
Vitamin A (retinol): Animal and fish liver, kidneys, eggs, milk and dairy products, oily fish, meat, margarine (which by law is fortified to contain as much vitamin A as is found in butter).
Beta-carotene: Dark green leafy vegetables and yellow orange fruits such as carrots, spinach, broccoli, spring greens, apricots, red and yellow peppers.
Vitamin A is easily destroyed by exposure to light. Beta-carotene is destroyed by heat and overcooking.

Vitamin B6
Natural vitamin B6 is really a group of six compounds that are converted to the active form—pyridoxine—in the body. Pyridoxine is essential for the proper functioning of over 60 enzymes. It is needed for the synthesis of genetic material, amino acids, sex hormones, brain chemicals, antibodies and for metabolising body stores of carbohydrate and essential fatty acids. Vitamin B6 is needed for production of hydrochloric acid in the stomach so that calcium can be absorbed. It is also necessary for cross-linking collagen (bone matrix material) and for breaking down homocysteine, an amino acid which in excess is linked with osteoporosis and heart disease.

EC RDA: 2mg.

Average daily intake: 4.5mg.

Research: Production of new bone is lower when there is a deficiency of vitamin B6. Dietary deficiency of vitamin B6 and low blood levels have been linked with osteoporosis and increased risk of hip fractures.

Possible signs of deficiency:

anaemia	anxiety
split lips	irritability
red, inflamed tongue	bloating
burning skin	tender breast
headache	osteoporosis
mild depression	

Good dietary sources:

yeast extract	meat
wholegrains	oily fish
liver	brown rice
soya products	green leafy vegetables
bananas	avocado
walnuts	egg yolk

Vitamin B6 is destroyed by cooking and by exposure to light.

Vitamin B12

Vitamin B12 contains the trace element cobalt, and is also called cobalamin. This is the only known function of cobalt in the human body. Vitamin B12 works together with folic acid to synthesise new copies of genetic material when cells divide, and in keeping nerve cells healthy. Vitamin B12 has only recently been found important to bone health—deficiency reduces the activity of bone-building cells (osteoblasts). Dietary vitamin B12 is absorbed in the lower part of the small intestine, but only if a carrier protein, intrinsic factor, is present. Intrinsic factor is made in the stomach and vitamin B12 deficiency sometimes develops because of lack of intrinsic factor or disease of the small intestine. Supplementation must then be given through regular injections.

EC RDA: 1mcg.

Average daily intake: 7mcg.

Possible signs of deficiency:

anaemia	clumsiness
smooth, sore tongue	poor memory
exhaustion	lack of concentration
menstrual disorders	confusion
numbness or tingling	depression
trembling	

Good dietary sources: Liver, kidney, oily fish (especially sardines), red meat, white fish, eggs, milk and dairy products.

Vitamin B12 is found only in animal-based foods. No natural plant products contain consistent amounts of vitamin B12, with the possible exception of some blue-green algae (vitamin B12 may not be present in an active form). Preparations of vitamin B12 made by bacterial fermentation—and therefore acceptable to vegetarians—are available.

Folic acid
Folic acid is involved in a wide number of metabolic reactions and in protein and sugar metabolism. It works together with vitamin B12 in the synthesis of genetic material during cell division and in keeping nerves healthy. The body stores very little folic acid, so dietary lack rapidly causes deficiency—it is probably the most widespread vitamin deficiency in developed countries.

Folic acid helps to prevent the build-up of an amino acid, homocysteine, which promotes both osteoporosis and coronary heart disease. Around one in ten people inherit higher than normal blood levels of homocysteine, which triples the risk of these diseases. One in 160,000 people have extremely high levels, with 30 times the risk of premature heart disease and osteoporosis.

EC RDA: 200mcg (400mcg–4mg if you are planning to conceive and during early pregnancy, to prevent certain developmental defects such as spina bifida).

Average daily intake: 245mcg (NB: 50 per cent of people get less than this).

Research: After the menopause, some women seem less able to process homocysteine so that levels build up to increase the risk of osteoporosis and coronary heart disease. High levels of homocysteine can be reduced by taking folic acid supplements (400mcg-650mcg per day) so that risk of heart disease and osteoporosis is reduced. Alcohol interferes with the metabolism of many vitamins and minerals, including folic acid, which is one reason why excess alcohol increases the risk of osteoporosis.

Possible signs of deficiency:

anaemia	forgetfulness
tiredness	confusion
muscle weakness and cramps	red, sore tongue
irritability	cracking at the corners of the
insomnia	mouth

VITAMINS AND MINERALS FOR BONE HEALTH

Good dietary sources:

green leafy vegetables (e.g. spinach, broccoli, Brussels sprouts, parsley)	liver
	beans
	wholemeal bread
yeast extract	kidney
soya products	dairy products
wholegrains	citrus fruit
nuts	eggs

Prolonged boiling destroys much of the folate present in green leafy vegetables. It is also destroyed by prolonged contact with light and air but can be protected by the antioxidant, vitamin C.

Vitamin C

Vitamin C (ascorbic acid) is essential for the synthesis of collagen, a major structural protein that makes up 30 per cent of bone volume. Vitamin C is therefore essential for healthy growth and repair of all tissues, including bone. Vitamin C has been found to stimulate bone-building cells (osteoblasts), enhance vitamin D activity and boost calcium absorption from the gut. Vitamin C is also involved in the metabolism of stress hormones, immune function and is a powerful antioxidant.

EC RDA: 60mg although increasing numbers of people feel that 200–2000mg are necessary for optimum health. A minimum daily intake of 10mg vitamin C is needed to prevent scurvy, although 20mg per day is needed for normal wound healing.

Average daily intake: 65mg (NB: 60 per cent of people get less than 60mg).

Research: Lack of vitamin C has been linked with osteoporosis, and bone abnormalities are found in scurvy due to faulty collagen production.

Possible signs of deficiency:

poor wound healing	easy bruising
dry, rough, scaly skin	loose teeth
broken thread veins in skin around hair follicles	inflamed, bleeding gums
	bleeding skin, eyes and nose
misshapen, tangled, brittle hair	weakness
	muscle and joint pain
scalp dryness	irritability
hair loss	depression
dry, fissured lips	

Good dietary sources: Blackcurrants, kiwi fruit, citrus fruit, mangoes, green peppers, strawberries, green sprouting vegetables (e.g. broccoli, sprouts, watercress, parsley).

Vitamin C is one of the most unstable vitamins and up to two thirds are lost by processing, cooking, storage and exposure to light. As vitamin C is water soluble, it is lost from vegetables by boiling in water although some can be reclaimed by using the water to make sauces, gravy, and so on. Better still, vegetables should be steamed or boiled with minimal water.

Vitamin D

Vitamin D is a vitamin that also acts as a hormone (calcitriol). It is needed for the absorption of dietary calcium and phosphate in the small intestine and for their deposition in bone. Under the regulation of parathyroid hormone, vitamin D also mobilises calcium and phosphorus from bone during remodelling.

Vitamin D is so essential for healthy bones that evolution has arranged for us to make small amounts in our skin on exposure to sunlight (see chapter 2).

EC RDA: 5mcg (10mcg is recommended over the age of 65 years).

Average daily intake: 3·4mcg (NB: 50 per cent of people get less than this).

Research: Lack of vitamin D causes deformed bones (rickets) in growing children and osteomalacia (softened bones) in adults. Lack of vitamin D can cause secondary hyperparathyroidism (high levels of parathyroid hormone) that in turn promotes osteoporosis. Four out of five people with hip fracture have evidence of vitamin D deficiency. Adding calcium supplements to the diet of elderly people reduces their risk of a vertebral fracture by 20 per cent, while giving them both calcium and vitamin D supplements reduces their risk of hip fracture by up to 40 per cent.

Possible signs of deficiency:

constipation	poor growth
muscle weakness	irritability
lowered immunity with	bone pain
increased susceptibility to	bone deformities (in rickets)
infections	deafness (in osteomalacia)

Good dietary sources: Oily fish (sardine, herring, mackerel, salmon, tuna), fish liver oils, fortified margarine, liver, eggs, fortified milk, butter (see also vitamin D tables in appendices).

Vitamin K
Vitamin K is a fat soluble vitamin that occurs in three different forms and is essential for normal blood clotting. It is needed for the synthesis of osteocalcin, a calcium-binding protein found in bone matrix. Vitamin K is as important for bone health as calcium.

EC RDA: None set. Requirements are thought to be around 1mcg per kilogram of body weight per day.

Average daily intake: 80mcg.

Research: Lack of vitamin K has been linked to thinning bones and osteoporosis. In one study, when vitamin K supplements were given to post-menopausal women, bone loss was reduced and their bones became stronger. Research suggests vitamin K supplement can reduce loss of bone calcium in post-menopausal women by up to 50 per cent.

Possible signs of deficiency: Prolonged bleeding time, easy bruising, recurrent nose bleeds, heavy periods, diarrhoea, osteoporosis

Good dietary sources:

cauliflower (richest source)	fish liver oils
dark green leafy vegetables	liver
kelp	tomatoes
yoghurt	meat
egg yolk	potatoes
alfalfa	pulses
safflower, rapeseed, soya and olive oils	

Bacteria in the gut produce some vitamin K which can be absorbed and used.

Vitamin K is found in green leafy vegetables such as cabbage and broccoli as well as in cauliflower, soya bean, rapeseed and olive oils.

WHAT SUPPLEMENTS DO YOU NEED?

Surveys in the UK estimate that only one in ten people get all the vitamins and minerals they need from their diet. Only:

- 40 per cent of people obtain the new EC recommended daily amounts (RDA) of 60mg vitamin C on a regular basis;
- 50 per cent of adults obtain enough vitamin B6;
- 40 per cent of people obtain recommended levels of dietary calcium.

Surveys also suggest that the average adult obtains only:

- 53 per cent of the RDA for zinc;
- 56 per cent of the RDA for vitamin D;
- 78 per cent of the RDA for magnesium.

Even if only one of these bone nutrients is in short supply, it may affect your metabolism or hormone balance to increase your risk of osteoporosis. Diet should always come first. By taking steps to ensure you eat a balanced diet that is rich in the important bone nutrients (for example, by drinking an extra pint of semi-skimmed or skimmed milk per day), you can help to optimise your bone health and prevent osteoporosis.

It is never too late—or too early—to start eating a bone-friendly diet. As a nutritional safety net, you may also wish to take a regular vitamin and mineral supplement. For general bone health, choose one that provides around 100 per cent of the recommended daily amount (RDA) of as many micronutrients as possible. Larger quantities of some micronutrients may be necessary, especially of calcium. Taking a vitamin and mineral supplement can reduce the risk of a fracture in post-menopausal women by at least a third.

CHAPTER 6

Osteoporosis Prevention During Pregnancy

Osteoporosis during pregnancy is increasingly common. To feed the hunger of developing fetal bones, calcium, magnesium and other minerals are leached from the mother's bones and teeth when dietary intake is poor—one reason why visits to the dentist are free at this time. This mineral drain is significant and can weaken the bones enough to cause fractures—hundreds of cases are thought to occur every year during the last three months of pregnancy or in the early breast-feeding period. Unfortunately, symptoms are often misdiagnosed as pregnancy-associated back pain or even as postnatal depression. In one case, a new mother's bone mass was found to have thinned to 50 per cent of the normal value for her age following delivery of her child.

Most women recover any lost bone mass spontaneously after childbirth so long as they have a high calcium intake and regular exercise. Affected mothers are strongly advised not to breast-feed, however, as this is a further drain on calcium stores.

Looking after your bones during pregnancy and breast-feeding

Pregnancy is a time when your need for vitamins and minerals increases enormously. A varied, wholefood diet is essential. In some cases, supplements are needed too.

At present, the only supplement universally recommended

during the time before conception and in pregnancy is folic acid (folate) to reduce the risk of some congenital abnormalities (neural tube defects) such as spina bifida.

The following table shows the new EC recommended daily amounts (RDAs) for adults, the UK reference nutrient intakes (RNIs) for women aged 19–50 yrs, together with the RNI recommended for pregnant women. The government reference nutrient intakes (RNIs) drawn up in 1991 accept that pregnant women need more vitamin A, thiamin (vitamin B1), riboflavin (vitamin B2), vitamin C, vitamin D and folic acid than non-pregnant women, but surprisingly claim that a woman needs no other vitamins or additional minerals during pregnancy. This is plainly ludicrous. In many cases, the recommended intakes for UK pregnant women are less than EC RDAs for non-pregnant adult women. These recommendations need urgent updating—not just for the health of mother and baby during pregnancy, but for the long-term health of the mother's bones and her future risk of osteoporosis.

Recommended daily intakes for adult women

NUTRIENT	NON-PREGNANT		PREGNANT	BREAST-FEEDING
	EC RDA	*RNI women (19–50 yrs)*	*RNI*	*RNI*
Vitamin A (retinol)	800mcg	600mcg	*+ 100mcg*	*+ 350mcg*
Vitamin B1 (thiamin)	1.4mg	0.8mg	*+ 0.1mg*	*+ 0.2mg*
Vitamin B2 (riboflavin)	1.6mg	1.1mg	*+ 0.3mg*	*+ 0.5mg*
Vitamin B3 (niacin)	18mg	13mg	*–*	*+ 2mg*
Vitamin B5 (pantothenic acid)	6mg	not set		

THE OSTEOPOROSIS PREVENTION GUIDE

NUTRIENT	NON-PREGNANT		PREGNANT	BREAST-FEEDING
	EC RDA	*RNI women (19–50 yrs)*	*RNI*	*RNI*
Vitamin B6 (pyridoxine)	*2mg*	*1.2mg*	–	–
Vitamin B12 (cyanocobalamin)	*1mcg*	*1.5mcg*	–	*+ 0.5mcg*
Folate	200mcg	200mcg	400mcg*	*+ 60mcg*
Biotin	150mcg	not set		
Vitamin C	60mg	40mg	*+ 10mg*	*+ 30mg*
Vitamin D	5mcg	**	10mcg	10mcg
Vitamin E	10mg	not set		
Calcium	800mg	700mg	–	*+ 550mg*
Copper	1.1mg	1.2mg	–	*+ 0.3mg*
Iodine	150mcg	140mcg	–	–
Iron	14mg	14.8mg	–	–
Magnesium	300mg	270mg	–	*+ 50mg*
Phosphorus	800mg	550mg	–	*+ 440mg*
Selenium	not set	60mcg	–	*+ 15mcg*
Zinc	15mg	7mg	–	*+ 6mg 0–4 months + 2.5mg thereafter assuming your baby has started to wean*

– No increase suggested.

* Plus increased intake of folate-rich food during preconceptual period until at least twelve weeks of pregnancy. Women who have previously had a child with a neural tube defect need increased intake of folate-rich foods plus 4mg (4000mcg) folate during the preconceptual care period until at least the twelfth week of pregnancy.

** No RNI needed for people who receive exposure to sunlight. An RNI of 10mcg is suggested for those confined indoors.

Minerals

Some researchers have suggested that women need the following additional minerals during pregnancy:

MINERAL	ADDITIONAL REQUIREMENTS SUGGESTED FOR PREGNANCY
Calcium	an extra 300mg per day
Chromium III	an extra 100mcg per day
Copper	an extra 0.5mg per day
Iron	an extra 10mg per day
Magnesium	an extra 100mg per day
Zinc	an extra 10mg per day

Calcium

The National Osteoporosis Society in the UK recommends the following calcium intakes:

non-pregnant women 19–44 years   1000mg per day
pregnant women   1200mg per day
breast-feeding mothers   1250mg per day

Calcium is needed during pregnancy for the growth and development of the baby's bones and teeth. It is also essential for muscle contraction, nerve conduction, blood coagulation, the production of energy and immunity. Babies born to mothers with a poor calcium intake tend to have a low birth weight and slow development. Lack of calcium is common during pregnancy and when breast-feeding as your requirements are increased. Human breast milk contains 25–35mg calcium per 100ml (150–210mg per pint).

Interestingly, calcium absorption from the gut seems to be more efficient during pregnancy. This is secondary to a natural increase in blood levels of vitamin D—without any obvious increase in intake or increased exposure to the sun.

Although breast-feeding results in significant loss of minerals from bone, these changes are reversible—even if you have several babies close together. New research suggests that bone loss during extended periods of breast-feeding and closely spaced pregnancies is unlikely to have a lasting effect on the bones of healthy, well-nourished women. This is very reassuring and suggests that by following a careful diet, women can continue to breast-feed—which is by far the best option for their baby—without worrying about their long-term risk of osteoporosis. A healthy diet, rich in vitamins, minerals and essential fatty acids is vital, however.

Magnesium

Magnesium is needed for every major biological process, from the synthesis of protein and DNA to glucose metabolism, energy production and enzyme function. It is essential for healthy tissues, including heart muscle and nerve cells. The National Research Council of America recommends a daily intake of 280mg magnesium for women, with an additional 40mg per day during pregnancy and an extra 60–75mg daily during lactation. The UK reference nutrient intake for adult women is 270mg per day. No increment is suggested during pregnancy, although an extra 50mg is recommended during lactation. Magnesium deficiency is common. The observed average daily intake of magnesium amongst British women is 237mg per day, which is significantly below the recommended level.

Lack of magnesium is exacerbated by pregnancy and some researchers believe deficiency contributes to miscarriage, premature delivery, painful contractions during labour and pregnancy-associated osteoporosis. To help prevent osteoporosis, ensure your magnesium intake is good during pregnancy and breast-feeding (see chapter 5).

Protein

Protein makes up around a third of the weight of your bones as it forms the framework on which calcium and other salts are deposited. The average non-pregnant adult woman needs around 45g (1¾oz) protein per day. During pregnancy, you need an extra 6g (¼oz) per day (total 51g or 2oz) and when breast-feeding, you need an extra 11g (½oz) protein during the first four months, and an extra 8g (¼oz) protein thereafter (assuming your baby has started to wean). To help prevent pregnancy-associated osteoporosis, make sure your intake of protein is adequate, although excessive amounts are not recommended (see chapter 4).

Essential fatty acids during pregnancy

You need more essential fatty acids (EFAs) during pregnancy than at any other time. They are vital for healthy cell membranes, development of the eyes, brain and nerve fibres as well as for hormone balance. EFAs are also converted into substances that reduce the risk of premature delivery, protect against high blood pressure during pregnancy and soften your cervix to trigger childbirth when the time is right.

Lack of essential fatty acids is common and the World Health Organisation (WHO) recently warned that the growing trend towards following a low fat diet means many pregnant women do not get all the essential fatty acids they need. A mum-to-be needs as much as 2g of EFAs per day.

If you are lacking in the EFAs, your baby will obtain all he needs from your body's richest store—your own brain. This has been suggested as one reason why some women become forgetful and have difficulty concentrating as their pregnancy progresses. By boosting your dietary intake of EFAs throughout pregnancy, you can help to optimise development of your baby's brain and eyes. You will also help to prevent osteoporosis, as EFAs help to boost calcium absorption from the gut, calcium loss in the urine and trigger increased calcium deposition in bone (see chapter 4). Increasing your intake of essential fatty acids, as well as boosting your calcium intake during pregnancy and breast-feeding, will help to protect against pregnancy-associated osteoporosis.

The richest sources of EFAs include oily fish (e.g. mackerel, herring, salmon, trout, sardines, pilchards), nuts, seeds, wholegrains and dark green leafy vegetables. Unless you eat 30g of nuts or seeds per day and 300g of oily fish per week, however, your diet may be lacking in these vital building blocks. Some research suggests that the balance of EFAs in rapeseed oil may be better for your baby's brain development than safflower or sunflower seed oils, so it may be worth switching to rapeseed oil for cooking.

Not everyone wants to make drastic changes to their diet, especially during pregnancy, and in any case, not everyone likes eating fish. If this is the case, it is worth considering taking a supplement containing EFAs from evening primrose and fish oils.

A supplement containing both these oils (Efanatal) has recently been launched especially for women who are planning a pregnancy, who are already pregnant or who are breast-feeding. This can be taken together with the folic acid supplements recommended before conception and for at least the first three months of pregnancy.

CHAPTER 7

Complementary Treatments to Help Strengthen Your Bones

Many women seek help from alternative therapists to help prevent or treat osteoporosis and other post-menopausal problems. There are many reasons for this, the most common being that you may not be able—or willing—to take hormone replacement therapy. When choosing an alternative practitioner, bear in mind that standards of training and experience vary widely. Where possible:

- Select a therapist on the basis of personal recommendation from a satisfied client whom you know and whose opinion you trust.
- Check what qualifications the therapist has, and check his or her standing with the relevant umbrella organisation for that therapy. The organisation will be able to tell you what training their members have undertaken and their code of ethics, and can refer you to qualified practitioners in your area.
- Find out how long your course of treatment will last and how much it is likely to cost.
- Ask how much experience the therapist has had in treating osteoporosis and what his or her success rate is.

The following complementary therapies have helped many men and women with a personal or family history of osteoporosis, but just as with orthodox medicine, not every treatment will suit every individual.

HERBALISM

Phytotherapy—the use of plant extracts for healing—is one of the most exciting areas of medical research. Traditional herbs have provided orthodox medicine with many powerful drugs, including aspirin (from the willow tree), digitalis (from the foxglove) and even potent new cancer treatments such as paclitaxel from the Pacific yew tree. Worldwide, specialists known as ethnobotanists are continually seeking new herbal treatments from among the traditional plants used by native healers. Different parts of different plants are used—roots, stems, flowers, leaves, bark, sap, fruit or seeds—depending on which has the highest concentration of active ingredient. These are dried and ground to produce a powder which is made into a tea, or packed into capsules for easy swallowing. Some extracts are also dissolved in alcohol to make a tincture.

Some herbs have medicinal properties that may help to prevent or treat osteoporosis. It is best to use them only after consulting a trained herbalist. Always check with both the herbalist and your usual doctor that any medications you are taking will not interact with any herbal prescriptions. Doses of each herb will vary depending on whether the preparation is dried, in the form of a tincture or concentrated or extracted. Always follow the dosage instructions on packets.

Some herbs contain plant hormones that mimic the action of natural human hormones in the body.(see chapter 4):

OESTROGENIC HERBS

Alfalfa (*Medicago sativa*)
Alfalfa is a common meadow plant used as cattle fodder.
Part used: Aerial parts and sprouting seeds.
What it does: Alfalfa contains plant hormones (isoflavones, coumarins) that mimic the effects of oestrogen in the body. It is used to help prevent and treat many menopausal symptoms, including:

- hot flushes
- night sweats
- low sex drive
- low mood
- osteoporosis

Cautions: Alfalfa is not recommended for those suffering from auto-immune diseases.

Black cohosh (*Cimicifuga racemosa*)
Black cohosh (also known as squaw root or black snake root) is a Native American remedy.
Part used: Dried root and rhizome (tuber).
What it does: Black cohosh has long been used to help gynaecological problems, especially those associated with the menopause. It contains isoflavones (oestrogen-like plant hormones) which help to boost oestrogen levels after the menopause. It also has sedative, relaxant and anti-inflammatory actions. It is used to regain normal hormone activity. Helpful for bone and joint problems such as rheumatic pains, rheumatoid arthritis, osteoarthritis and osteoporosis. Used to help prevent and treat many gynaecological symptoms such as:

- painful or irregular periods
- uterine cramps (including labour pains)
- sex hormone imbalances
- pre-menstrual syndrome
- hot flushes

Cautions: As black cohosh stimulates the womb, it should not be taken during early pregnancy (seek advice).

Comfrey (*Symphytum officinale*)
Comfrey is also known as knitbone. It has a reputation for helping to mend broken bones and gains its popular name from the Latin *conferva* meaning 'boiled together'. Its botanical name, Symphytum, comes from the Greek meaning 'to unite'.
Part used: Leaves and flowering tops.
What it does: Comfrey contains allantoin, a substance that stimulates division and multiplication of damaged cells, especially in bone, ligament and muscle. It is traditionally used to hasten the healing of bruises, sprains and fractures and is sometimes prescribed to help osteoporosis—especially where an osteoporotic fracture has occurred. It also contains steroidal saponins that have a weak oestrogenic action.
Cautions: Do not take preparations containing comfrey root by mouth, as the root contains substances (pyrrolizidine alkaloids) that may be toxic to the liver. Root preparations may be used on the skin, however, to help acne, boils, wound healing and varicose ulcers. Comfrey is a restricted herb in Australia and New Zealand.

Dong quai (*Angelica sinensis*)
Chinese angelica—also known as dong quai or sometimes dang gui—is a traditional Chinese medicinal herb also used in cooking for its sweet flavour.
Part used: Dried rhizome.
What it does: Dong quai contains a powerful plant hormone, betasitosterol, which helps to boost oestrogen levels after the menopause. It is used to help prevent and relieve menopausal symptoms of hot flushes and night sweats, as well as to help protect against osteoporosis. It is also used to:

- treat painful or irregular periods
- stimulate circulation to the hands and feet

- treat anaemia
- ease constipation
- boost liver function

Cautions: Dong quai is a uterine stimulant, so avoid regular or large doses in pregnancy. Do not take if you have high blood pressure.

False unicorn (*Chamaelirium luteum* or *Helonias dioica*)
False unicorn is a native North American plant also known as helonias, blazing star and fairy wand.
Part used: Root.
What it does: False unicorn is used to treat gynaecological problems. It contains plant hormones (steroidal saponins) similar to those found in ginseng, which act as building blocks for making oestrogen. It therefore helps to stimulate secretion of natural oestrogen from the ovaries. It encourages a normal menstrual cycle and has also been used:

- to treat menopausal symptoms, endometriosis and ovarian cysts;
- to boost ovarian function after stopping long-term oral contraceptives;
- as a uterine tonic;
- to help induce menstruation in women with irregular or absent periods;
- to help reduce fluid retention;
- to help prevent miscarriage;
- to ease morning sickness in pregnancy;
- for tiredness, backache and low mood associated with the menopause;
- to treat and prevent osteoporosis.

It can take several months for false unicorn to have an effect so it is usually taken for long courses.
Cautions: High doses can cause nausea and vomiting.

Ginseng (*Panax ginseng*)

Korean (or Chinese) ginseng has been used in Chinese medicine for over 7,000 years. In the East, ginseng is taken in a two weeks on, two weeks off cycle. It should not normally be taken for longer than six weeks without a break of at least two to three weeks.

Part used: Root.

What it does: Ginseng contains steroid building blocks (panaxosides; ginsenosides; sterols) similar to human sex hormones. It is used to help people adapt to stressful situations (adaptogen) and improves physical and mental energy. Research suggests it boosts immunity, stimulates proliferation of cells and prolongs their life. It normalises glucose and hormone levels and is used to help prevent and treat menopausal symptoms such as:

- hot flushes
- low mood
- lack of energy
- lowered blood pressure
- insomnia
- low sex drive
- osteoporosis

Cautions: Make sure you buy a good quality product from a reputable company—cheap versions may contain very little active ingredient. Analysis of 50 ginseng products sold in 11 countries found that six contained no ginseng at all, and in the others content of ginsenosides varied from 1.9 per cent to 9 per cent by weight.

Do not take ginseng if you have high blood pressure (can make hypertension worse) or suffer from an oestrogen-dependent condition such as some gynaecological cancers. Avoid in pregnancy (except under medical advice). It is best to avoid taking other stimulants such as caffeine-containing products and drinks (tea, coffee and cola) while taking ginseng.

Vitamin C may neutralise ginseng, and some practitioners suggest leaving eight hours between the two.

Liquorice (*Glycyrrhiza glabra*)

Liquorice is a popular sweetmeat that contains glycyrrhizin, a chemical 50 times sweeter than sugar. Liquorice also has medicinal actions and is sometimes referred to as the 'grand-father of herbs'.

Part used: Root.

What it does: Contains isoflavones that have an oestrogenic action. Reduces the breakdown of natural steroid hormones (including oestrogen) in the liver, so that levels are raised. Also used to reduce inflammation, treat liver problems, treat respiratory or gastric problems and to boost the function of the adrenal glands. The oestrogenic effect can help prevent or treat menopausal problems including osteoporosis.

Cautions: If you suffer from high blood pressure, avoid eating excessive amounts of liquorice—it can make hypertension worse. Do not take in pregnancy or when breast-feeding. Do not take if you are also taking prescribed digoxin (digitalis).

Pfaffia (*Pfaffia paniculata*)

Pfaffia is the root of a Rain Forest plant that is often referred to as the Brazilian ginseng, although it is unrelated to the Oriental varieties.

Part used: Root.

What it does: Pfaffia is a powerful adaptogen which helps the immune system adapt to improve physical and mental stamina in times of stress. It is regarded as a panacea for all ills, as well as a sustaining food by local Indians who call it *para todo*—'for everything'. It is a rich source of vitamins, minerals, amino acids and plant hormones (phytosterols) that act as building blocks for oestrogen. Pfaffia is used to help prevent and treat many gynaecological problems, including:

- pre-menstrual syndrome
- menopausal symptoms
- symptoms related to the oral contraceptive pill
- the prevention and treatment of osteoporosis

Pfaffia can be difficult to get hold of—in the UK it is obtainable from the importers, Rio Trading, on 01273 570987.
Cautions: Pfaffia should not be taken by pregnant women.

Red Clover (*Trifolium pratense*)
Red clover is a common weed used by farmers to fix nitrogen in soil and make hay.
Part used: Flowerheads, leaves and sometimes sprouted seeds.
What it does: Red clover contains plant hormones (sitosterols; flavonoids) that act as building blocks for making oestrogen and other sex hormones. It is used for its oestrogenic effects in helping to prevent and treat menopausal symptoms including osteoporosis. It is popular for treating skin problems and is also said to have a contraceptive effect in sheep.
Cautions: None

Sage (*Salvia officinalis*)
Sage is a general panacea whose botanical name comes from the Latin *salvia*, meaning 'the healing plant'. It is a popular culinary herb but also has important medicinal uses. Purple sage is the most potent member of the family and the type preferred by herbalists.
Part used: Leaves.
What it does: Sage contains flavonoids and a volatile oil, thujone, that are oestrogenic. Sage is so oestrogenic that it can reduce production of breast milk. It is also used to:

- help irregular, scanty periods
- encourage menstruation
- reduce hot flushes and night sweats

- help the body adapt to the menopause
- prevent osteoporosis

Cautions: Do not use during pregnancy or breast-feeding. In excess, may be toxic.

HOMOEOPATHY

Homoeopathy is based on the belief that natural substances can boost the body's own healing powers to relieve symptoms and signs of illness. Natural substances are selected which, if used full strength, would produce in a healthy person symptoms similar to those it is designed to treat. This is the first principle of homoeopathy, that 'like cures like'.

The second major principle is that increasing dilution of a solution has the opposite effect of increasing its potency—that is, 'less cures more'. By diluting noxious and even poisonous substances many millions of times, their healing properties are enhanced while their undesirable side effects are lost.

On the centesimal scale, dilutions of 100^{-6} are described as potencies of 6c, dilutions of 100^{-30} are written as a potency of 30c, and so on. To illustrate just how diluted these substances are, a dilution of 12c (100^{-12}) is comparable to a pinch of salt dissolved in the same amount of water as is found in the Atlantic Ocean!

Homoeopathy is thought to work in a dynamic way, boosting your body's own healing powers. The principles that like cures like and less cures more are difficult concepts to accept, yet convincing trials have shown that homoeopathy is significantly better than a placebo in treating many chronic (long-term) conditions, including hayfever, asthma and rheumatoid arthritis.

Homoeopathic remedies should ideally be taken on their own, without eating or drinking for at least 30 minutes before or after. Tablets should also be taken without handling—tip them into the lid of the container, or onto a teaspoon to transfer

97

them into your mouth. Then suck or chew them, don't swallow them whole.

Homoeopathic treatments are prescribed according to your symptoms rather than any particular disease, so two patients with the same label of osteoporosis, for example, who have different symptoms will need different homoeopathic treatments.

Homoeopathic remedies may be prescribed by a medically-trained homoeopathic doctor on the normal NHS prescription form and dispensed by homoeopathic pharmacists for the usual prescription charge or exemptions. Alternatively, you can consult a private homoeopathic practitioner or buy remedies direct from the pharmacist.

It is best to see a trained homoeopath who can assess your constitutional type, personality, lifestyle, family background, likes and dislikes as well as your symptoms before deciding which treatment is right for you. The following remedies to help prevent or treat osteoporosis are sometimes suggested. Don't be surprised if your symptoms initially get worse before they get better; persevere through this common reaction to treatment—therapists believe it is a good sign which shows the remedy is working.

Calc. phos (*Calcarea phosphorica*)
Calc. phos is a homoeopathic tissue salt used to help bone and teeth problems, including the prevention and treatment of osteoporosis. It is also used to help overcome weakness, exhaustion and fatigue.

Ruta grav (*Ruta graveolens*)
Homoeopathic Ruta grav is made from the bitter juice of the herb, rue. It is used to help conditions in which the lining of the bone (periosteum) is bruised, with deep aching pain, rheumatism, painful tendons or sciatica. It is sometimes used to help treat osteoporosis where the bone has been damaged.

TREATMENTS TO HELP STRENGTHEN YOUR BONES

Theridion (*Theridion curassavicum*)
Theridion is a homoeopathic remedy made from a venomous orange spider. It mainly acts on the nerves, spine and bones and is useful for helping people with spinal osteoporosis.

Bryonia (*Bryonia alba*)
Bryonia is a homoeopathic root extract from a common plant, wild hops. The root itself is highly poisonous. When diluted to homoeopathic strength, it is used to treat painful conditions that come on slowly, including influenza, headaches, osteoarthritis, rheumatism and other bone problems, including osteoporosis.

Homoeopathic hormones
Homoeopathic hormones (oestrogen, progesterone, testosterone and/or oestradiol) may be prescribed, usually depending on the results of saliva tests. The tests are taken every three days throughout a normal menstrual cycle (or for a four-week period after the menopause) to measure oestrogen, progesterone, and testosterone levels; results are then plotted on a graph to show what hormone changes are linked with the menstrual cycle, menopausal symptoms or the presence of osteoporosis. Homoeopathic progesterone may be given in the form of homoeopathic wild yam cream.

AROMATHERAPY

Aromatherapy essential oils can strongly influence your moods, because the part of the brain that detects smell messages from the nose (olfactory bulbs) is closely linked with your emotional centre in a part of the brain called the limbic system. Oils are also absorbed from the skin into the circulation and can have powerful effects on the body. Unless otherwise stated, aromatherapy oils should always be used in a diluted form by adding to a carrier oil—some neat oils will irritate tissues. Use to massage into the skin, add to bathwater or diffuse into the air to scent your room. Oestrogenic oils include:

- clary sage (do not drink alcohol during treatment as this may trigger nightmares)
- fennel
- star anise
- tarragon

The last two essential oils are not easy to find except by mail order (see Useful Addresses).

ACUPUNCTURE

Acupuncture is based on the belief that life energy (Chi or Qi) flows through your body along twelve different channels called meridians. When this energy flow becomes blocked, symptoms of illness are triggered. By inserting fine needles into specific acupuncture points overlying these meridians, blockages are overcome and the flow of Chi corrected or altered to relieve symptoms. Altogether, there are 365 acupoints in the body and your therapist will select which points to use depending on your individual symptoms. Fine, disposable needles are used which cause little if any discomfort. You may notice a slight pricking sensation, or an odd tingling buzz as the needle is inserted a few millimetres into the skin. The needles are usually left in place for up to 20 minutes, and may be twiddled periodically. Sometimes, a small cone of dried herbs is ignited and burned near the active acupoint to warm the skin. This is known as moxibustion. The best known effect of Chi manipulation is local anaesthesia. Research suggests that acupuncture causes the release of natural, heroin-like chemicals that act as natural painkillers. Acupuncture can help most conditions including osteoporosis, menopausal symptoms and bone pain.

Acupressure is similar to acupuncture, but instead of

inserting needles at selected points along the meridians, they are stimulated using firm thumb pressure or fingertip massage. The best known example of acupressure is Shiatsu massage. This is particularly effective if combined with aromatherapy essential oils for a therapeutic massage.

ALEXANDER TECHNIQUE

The Alexander Technique is based on the belief that poor posture and faulty body movements contribute to disease. By teaching people to stand and move correctly, without undue stress, the Alexander Technique aims to improve ill health. Its principles are used to treat a wide variety of conditions, including osteoporosis.

BIOELECTROMAGNETIC THERAPY

Bioelectromagnetic therapy accesses the body's electric and magnetic fields through acupuncture points on the surface of the skin. Some types of illness and pain are associated with imbalances in these biological electric and magnetic fields. The body's cells—including those in bone—are bathed in a fluid containing a variety of dissolved chemicals and salts. Once dissolved, these separate into particles known as ions which carry an electric charge. The movement of positively and negatively charged ions means that every cell acts like a mini battery to produce a minute electrical charge. The electrical charge across your cell membranes, known as the membrane potential, varies from -9mV to -100 mV in different tissues. The movement of electrically charged ions in and out of cells is the main source of the body's electrical field. Interestingly, the active transport of sodium and potassium ions in and out of cells is one of the main energy-using metabolic processes occurring in the body. It accounts for 33 per cent of energy (in the form of glucose fuel) used by cells and 70 per cent of energy used by nerves. In osteoporosis, there is a gross mineral deficiency in bone. Bone cells that are weakened through lack of calcium and other essential minerals will have electrical imbalances across their cell membranes as a result of ionic imbalances. The flow of electrically charged ions in and out of cells creates a magnetic field. In osteoporosis, the minute magnetic field generated by the movement of electrically charged ions across the bone cell membranes will be abnormal as well.

Bioelectromagnetic therapy uses small patches (e.g. Acumed) that contain a rare earth magnet (an alloy of neodymium, iron and boron) coated with purified zinc and surrounded with tiny copper spheres. These elements are pre-aligned and attached to self-adhesive microporous tape to ensure the correct magnetic pole is in contact with the body. These patches generate three different bioelectromagnetic fields:

- magnetic—with the south pole facing away from the skin;
- micro-electric—due to copper and zinc forming a battery bridged by moisture from the skin;
- induced electric current—due to the magnetic field acting on the copper microspheres.

These fields interact to produce pulsations of energy that are more effective than using a continuous signal. The patches are applied to clean, dry skin on acupuncture points around affected bones (e.g. spine, hip or the site of an osteoporotic fracture). They are then left on the skin, undisturbed, for five to seven days. They can be worn during all normal daily activities, including bathing and showering. After five to seven days the patches should be gently peeled away and discarded. New magnets can be resited as necessary, but it is usually beneficial to 'rest' for one or two days before restarting treatment.

Bioelectromagnetic therapy will help to boost blood circulation through bone and surrounding tissues. Blood contains iron and copper as well as dissolved ions and is a powerful conductor of electric and magnetic currents. In 1954, for example, Linus Pauling received the Nobel Prize in Chemistry partly for discovering the magnetic properties of haemoglobin, the pigment found in red blood cells. As red blood cells pass through small capillaries under the electromagnetic patch, they travel through a magnetic field which inevitably produces a small electric current. This boosts blood flow and strengthens the circulation. Improved blood flow in turn increases the amount of oxygen, glucose and nutrients available to cells, helping to keep them healthy. Pulsed magnetic fields produced by the patches also seem to stabilise genetic material and enhance its synthesis as well as activating metabolic reactions. These two effects combined seem to boost healing and repair of damaged tissues such as osteoporotic bone. The healing effect has even been shown to stimulate shrinking and re-modelling of the bony protuberances (osteophytes) seen in osteoarthritis.

Acumed bioelectromagnetic patches are available in some UK health stores and large supermarkets, or through mail order (see Useful Addresses).

CHIROPRACTIC

Chiropractic is a technique based on the theory that disease is due to poor body alignment and abnormal nerve functioning. The body compensates by changing its alignment which causes ill health. Diagnosis is usually made by X-ray. Chiropractors use their hands to manipulate the spine with rapid, direct thrusts. This increases the 'nerve supply' and corrects poor alignment. Chiropractic is commonly used to help osteoporosis, when more gentle movements are used.

NATUROPATHY

Naturopathists advise regular exercise such as swimming, good protein intake and a wholefood diet containing nuts and seeds, grains and pulses. Biochemic tissue salts such as Calc. fluor. and Calc. phos. may be prescribed. Supplements containing calcium, vitamin D and other minerals and trace elements are also used. These may be combined with nettle extracts which are rich in calcium and which are also thought to improve the uptake of minerals from the gut.

NUTRITIONAL THERAPY

Nutritional therapists advise reducing excess intakes of caffeine, phosphorus, protein, salt and sugar while maintaining intakes of magnesium, calcium, boron, zinc and vitamins D and K. Regular exercise is also recommended.

OSTEOPATHY

Osteopathy is a method of diagnosis and treatment based on the mechanical structure of the body. Gentle manipulation corrects poor alignment and improves body function. Osteopathy is helpful for bone and joint problems, including osteoporosis.

T'AI-CHI CHU'AN

T'ai-chi Chu'an involves a series of graceful body movements that help to improve posture, flexibility and balance. This technique can help to strengthen bones through its gentle exercise, and also reduce the likelihood of falling so that the risk of a fracture is reduced. T'ai-chi Chu'an also helps you adapt to a physical problem such as osteoporosis while maintaining a positive, creative, youthful and relaxed outlook on life.

YOGA

Yoga is an oriental technique that involves postural exercises, breathing techniques and relaxation. Therapists believe that osteoporosis can be combated by more efficient breathing. Diaphragmatic breathing is said to help you adapt to changes in bone structure.

CHAPTER 8

Bone-Building Recipes

In this chapter you will find 80 delicious recipes rich in bone-building ingredients such as essential fatty acids, plant hormones, vitamins, minerals and trace elements.

I have not suggested recipes for puddings. This is because the best, most healthy desserts consist of fresh fruit, Bio yoghurt, cheese and plain wholemeal biscuits. By using the recipes given here, mostly based on the renowned Mediterranean diet, you will not only be helping to prevent osteoporosis, but will also be reducing your risk of coronary heart disease, high blood pressure and stroke.

When serving the dishes below, concentrate on accompanying them with bone-building side dishes, such as:

- salads sprinkled with chopped fresh herbs, nuts and seeds;
- green leafy vegetables (e.g. curly kale, spinach, broccoli) seasoned with sesame seed oil, walnut oil and sesame seeds;
- vegetables (e.g. carrots, courgettes, peas) laced with yoghurt, lemon juice and sesame seeds.

The tables at the end of this book, showing which foods are high in calcium, magnesium, zinc and vitamin D, will provide a useful guide. Try not to add salt, but if you feel this is essential, use mineral-rich rock salt.

Enjoy.

MISCELLANEOUS

Fruit and Nut Seed Muesli

Makes 700g (1lb 12oz) of muesli mix. Top with semi-skimmed milk and low fat fromage frais or yoghurt.

50g (2oz) rolled oats	50g (2oz) walnuts, chopped
50g (2oz) toasted wheatflakes	25g (1oz) brazil nuts, chopped
50g (2oz) rye flakes	25g (1oz) hazelnuts, chopped
50g (2oz) barley flakes	50g (2oz) pine nuts
50g (2oz) bran buds/flakes	25g (1oz) sunflower seeds
100g (4oz) dried apricots, chopped	25g (1oz) pumpkin seeds
50g (2oz) dried dates, chopped	25g (1oz) sesame seeds
50g (2oz) dried figs, chopped	25g (1oz) poppy seeds

Mix together all ingredients and store in an air-tight container. Shake well before weighing out each serving as the bran and small seeds will tend to settle.

Mixed Seeds and Nuts to Sprinkle on Salads

50g (2oz) sunflower seeds, toasted and/or raw	50g (2oz) pine kernels
50g (2oz) pumpkin seeds, toasted and/or raw	50g (2oz) sesame seeds, toasted
100g (4oz) mixed unsalted nuts	50g (2oz) poppy seeds

Mix well. Sprinkle onto salads, rice, main meals—whenever and as often as you can.

Kedgeree (serves 4)

400g (14oz) cooked brown rice

4 hard-boiled eggs, chopped

300g (11oz) flaked smoked haddock (colouring free)

4 tbsp fresh parsley, chopped

4 tbsp fresh coriander leaf, chopped

4 spring onions, finely chopped

4 tsp garam massala (or freshly ground curry powder)

150g (5oz) low fat fromage frais

Freshly ground black pepper

Garnish: watercress, grated nutmeg and fresh lemon juice.

Mix all ingredients well and serve piled onto a platter, garnished with watercress, grated nutmeg and sprinkled with lemon juice.

SAUCES, DIPS AND DRESSINGS

Pesto Sauce

50g (2oz) fresh basil leaves, washed and dried without bruising

50g (2oz) pine kernels or walnuts, chopped

3 cloves garlic, crushed

180ml (6fl oz) extra virgin olive oil

30g (1oz) Parmesan cheese, freshly grated

30g (1oz) Pecorino cheese (or more Parmesan), freshly grated

Rock salt and freshly ground black pepper

Either (if you like a smooth sauce):
Place the basil, salt, pepper and garlic in a blender and reduce to a smooth, green purée. Add the pine kernels or walnuts and cheese and blend slightly. Drizzle in the olive oil until you have a smooth, creamy textured sauce. Season to taste.
Or (if you like a coarser textured sauce):
Grind the basil leaves against the side of a marble pestle with a wooden mortar. Add the garlic and crush together with a little olive oil. Add the pine kernels and crush together with

more olive oil. Pound in the cheese and the remaining olive oil. Season to taste.

Pesto can be sweetened slightly by adding the mashed flesh of one grilled beef tomato to the recipe—to make red pesto sauce.

Stir into soups, stews or use as a delicious dressing on pasta and potatoes.

Greek Almond and Garlic Relish

Traditionally used to enliven plain, grilled fish or boiled prawns. Can also be spooned over vegetables and potatoes.

4 large cloves garlic, crushed	30ml (1fl oz) white wine
150ml (5fl oz) extra virgin	vinegar
olive oil	Rock salt and freshly ground
1 slice white bread, de-crusted	black pepper
100g (4oz) ground almonds	

Soak the bread in the vinegar. Crush the garlic to a purée in a pestle and mortar or blender. Stir in the oil, a little at a time. Blend in the vinegar-soaked bread and ground almonds. Season to taste.

Walnut Sauce

Can be used to stuff pasta shapes, dress pasta or as a dip for vegetable crudités.

225g (8oz) walnuts	2 tbsp extra virgin olive oil
1 slice white bread, de-crusted	2 tbsp walnut oil
45ml (2fl oz) semi-skimmed	4 tbsp thick fromage frais
milk	Rock salt and freshly ground
2 cloves garlic, crushed	black pepper

Soak the bread in the milk, then squeeze out excess moisture. Crush the walnuts in a pestle or blender until finely ground. Blend in the bread, crushed garlic, oils and fromage frais. Mix well to achieve a homogeneous sauce. If you are using the sauce to dress, rather than stuff, pasta and it seems too dry, add a little extra walnut or olive oil. Season to taste.

Italian Olive Relish

A Sicilian olive sauce used to accompany grilled fish or meat. This is best made one or two days in advance so that the flavours can infuse.

400g (14oz) green olives, stoned and crushed
3 tbsp fresh dill weed, finely chopped
1 tbsp chives, finely chopped
Newly sprouted tops of six mint sprigs, finely chopped
4 cloves garlic, crushed
1cm (½ in) ginger root, finely chopped

2 celery sticks, finely chopped
½ red chilli pepper, deseeded and finely chopped
10 tbsp extra virgin olive oil
5 tbsp balsamic vinegar
1 tbsp acacia honey
Rock salt and freshly ground black pepper

Place all the ingredients in an earthenware bowl and mix thoroughly. If preferred, blend to a smooth paste in a liquidiser. Cover and leave to stand, if possible, for 24 hours. Stir again just before serving.

Raita (serves 4)

This eastern Mediterranean dip can be served as a salad, a sauce with grilled fish or curries and as a dip with vegetable crudités. It may also be diluted with chilled water and served as a summer soup.

1 medium cucumber, peeled and grated
3 cloves garlic, crushed
2 tbsp fresh mint, chopped
1 tbsp chives, chopped
1 tbsp freshly squeezed lemon juice

500g (1lb 2oz) strained Greek (or low fat) yoghurt
1 tsp acacia honey (optional)
Rock salt and freshly ground black pepper
Freshly ground nutmeg to taste

Mix all ingredients together in an earthenware bowl. Season with salt and black pepper to taste. Serve topped with freshly ground nutmeg.

Hummus

This chickpea and sesame dip is often served with vegetable crudités or as part of a Greek meze course. Also delicious on toast.

The dried chickpeas should be soaked in water overnight — or until their weight has more or less doubled.

150g (5oz) dried chickpeas, soaked overnight	120g (4oz) tahini (sesame) paste
Freshly squeezed juice and zest of 2 lemons	3 tbsp extra virgin olive oil
3 cloves garlic, crushed	Rock salt and freshly ground black pepper

Garnish: chopped parsley or paprika pepper

After soaking the chickpeas, change their water and simmer for 1½ hours, or until soft. Drain, saving the liquor residue. Put 5 tbsp cooking liquor in a blender with the olive oil, lemon juice, zest and garlic. Start to blend. Slowly add the chickpeas and tahini paste. If the blender clogs, add more liquor until a grainy, creamy purée is obtained. Season to taste. More olive oil or tahini paste can be added to vary the flavour as desired.

SALADS AND STARTERS

Mixed Leaf Salad with Feta Cheese and Hazelnuts (serves 4)

225g (8oz) mixed salad leaves	120g (4oz) newly sprouted pulses (e.g. bean shoots, alfalfa)
Handful of fresh, flat leaf parsley	
Handful of fresh coriander leaves	50g (2oz) roasted hazelnuts, crushed
50g (2oz) crumbled Feta cheese	

Dressing

4 tbsp hazelnut, extra virgin or walnut oil	1 tsp whole grain mustard
2 tbsp fresh lemon juice or herb vinegar	1 clove garlic, crushed
	1 tsp acacia honey
	Rock salt and freshly ground black pepper

Combine all the salad ingredients in a serving bowl and mix well, being careful not to bruise the leaves. Mix the salad dressing ingredients thoroughly. Season to taste. Pour the dressing over the salad, toss and serve immediately.

Greek Salad (serves 4)
A traditional Greek salad to serve as a side dish with pitta bread or boiled new potatoes and fish.

225g (8oz) mixed green salad leaves
8 whole radishes, trimmed
12 black olives, rinsed and stoned
12 green olives, rinsed and stoned
1 red onion, thickly sliced and separated into rings
1 red sweet pepper, de-seeded and cut into strips
1 green pepper, deseeded and cut into strips
¼ cucumber, thinly sliced
8–12 sweet cherry tomatoes
1 can anchovy fillets, drained and rinsed
225g (8oz) Greek Feta cheese

Dressing
4 tbsp extra virgin olive oil
1 tbsp fresh lemon juice
1 tbsp red wine vinegar
1 clove garlic, crushed
1 tsp whole grain mustard
1 tsp acacia honey
1 tbsp mixed fresh herbs, chopped (e.g. parsley, basil, oregano, thyme)
Rock salt and freshly ground black pepper

Arrange all the salad ingredients except the anchovies in a large, wooden bowl. To make the vinaigrette, place all dressing ingredients in a screw-top jar and shake vigorously. Pour over the salad ingredients and toss well. Decorate the salad with a lattice of anchovy fillets. Garnish with grated Parmesan cheese and coriander leaves.

Green Lentil, Ginger and Coriander Salad (serves 4)
This salad is best made while the cooked, green lentils are still hot so that the flavours infuse. Serve warm with fish

or chicken dishes, or allow to chill when the flavours have marinaded. The amount of ginger, lemon juice and coriander leaves can be varied according to personal preference.

225g (8oz) green lentils	30ml (1fl oz) freshly squeezed
600ml (1 pt) water	lemon (or lime) juice
1 large carrot, grated	1 tbsp coriander seed, crushed
1 medium onion, finely	1–2 tbsp fresh coriander
chopped	leaves, finely chopped
2 cloves garlic, crushed	2.5cm (1 in) fresh root ginger,
45ml (2fl oz) extra virgin	peeled and finely chopped
olive oil	

Simmer the lentils in water for around 30 minutes, until they are cooked but still firm. Add the grated carrot and cook for a further five minutes. Drain. Heat half the olive oil and fry the onion, garlic and crushed coriander seeds until beginning to colour. Add the fried onion mixture and the remaining ingredients to the drained lentils. Mix well and season to taste. If serving hot, keep warm for flavours to infuse. Garnish with grated Parmesan cheese and coriander leaves.

Salad Niçoise (serves 4)
This dish from Nice makes a satisfying and filling lunch, or a classic hors d'ouevres.

450g (1lb) French green	8 small, new boiled potatoes
beans, topped and tailed	(cold), halved
2 little gem lettuce hearts	8 sweet cherry tomatoes
200g (7oz) canned tuna fish in	8 black olives, stoned and
olive oil, drained	halved
2 hard-boiled eggs, shelled	1 small onion, thinly sliced
and chopped	and separated into rings
1 small can anchovy fillets,	Several flat parsley leaves
drained and rinsed	Several coriander leaves
	A few chives

Dressing

4 tbsp extra virgin olive oil
1-2 tbsp balsamic vinegar
1 clove garlic, crushed
1 tsp whole grain mustard
1 tsp acacia honey

1 tbsp fresh parsley, finely
chopped
1 tbsp fresh basil, finely
chopped
Rock salt and freshly ground
black pepper

Cut the green beans in half lengthways, and steam for 5–10 minutes until tender but still crisp. Drain, and plunge into icy cold water. Place all the salad dressing ingredients in a screw-top jar. Season and shake well. Line a salad bowl with lettuce leaves. Arrange the potatoes and green beans on top. Pile the tuna fish into the middle of the bowl. Decorate round the edges with chopped egg, black olives and tomatoes. Make a lattice of anchovy fillets over the top. Shake the salad dressing and drizzle all over. Garnish with grated Parmesan cheese, coriander and flat parsley leaves.

Tuna and Pasta Salad

Serve four as a starter or two as a lunch dish with crispy bread.

225g (8oz) mixed salad leaves
200g (7oz) flaked tuna meat,
preferably fresh or canned
in olive oil (drained)
225g (8oz) cooked,
wholemeal pasta shapes
100g (4oz) low fat, natural
cottage cheese

1 beef tomato, chopped
2 spring onions, chopped
2 tbsp fresh parsley, chopped
1 tbsp freshly squeezed lemon
juice
4 tbsp low fat fromage frais
Freshly ground black pepper

Mix all ingredients except the salad leaves together and season well. Arrange the salad leaves in a bowl and top with the tuna and pasta mixture. Garnish with grated Parmesan cheese and watercress.

Mediterranean Bean Salad (serves 4)

225g (8oz) dried haricot or cannellini beans, soaked overnight
600ml (1 pt) water
1 carrot, grated
1 bay leaf
1 sprig rosemary

1 sprig thyme
4 spring onions, finely chopped
1 tbsp fresh parsley, chopped
1 tbsp fresh basil, chopped
1 tbsp fresh tarragon, chopped
1 tbsp fresh oregano, chopped

Dressing
4 tbsp extra virgin olive oil
1 tbsp balsamic (or tarragon) vinegar
1 tsp whole grain mustard

1 tsp acacia honey
Rock salt and freshly ground black pepper

Bring the water to the boil. Add the beans, bayleaf, rosemary and thyme. Cover and simmer for 1½–2 hours until cooked. Top up with water if necessary to prevent boiling dry. Drain and discard the boiled herbs. Mix the salad dressing ingredients in a screw-top jar and shake well. Season to taste. Combine the beans, grated carrot, chopped spring onions and remaining herbs. Pour the dressing over. Mix well and allow to marinade before serving.

Aromatic Bean Salad (serves 4)

400g (14oz) cooked, mixed beans
1 beef tomato, chopped
2 cloves garlic, crushed
2 tbsp fresh coriander leaves, chopped
A few coriander seeds, crushed
2 tbsp fresh parsley, chopped

2 tbsp freshly squeezed lemon juice
2 tbsp freshly squeezed orange juice
4 tbsp low fat fromage frais
Rock salt and freshly ground black pepper

Mix together all ingredients and season well.

Bean and Fennel Salad (serves 4)

400g (14oz) cooked flageolet
beans
200g (7oz) Florence fennel,
chopped into matchsticks
100g (4oz) carrot, grated
1 tsp fresh ginger root, grated
2 tbsp fresh dill, chopped

2 tbsp fresh parsley, chopped
2 tbsp freshly squeezed lemon
juice
2 cloves garlic, crushed
1 tbsp extra virgin olive oil
Freshly ground black pepper

Mix together all ingredients and allow to marinade for several hours before eating.

Pasta Salad with Apple, Cheese, Celery, Walnuts and Grapes (serves 4)

225g (8oz) mixed leaf salad
350g (12oz) cold, cooked
pasta
100g (4oz) low fat cottage
cheese
50g (2oz) Parmesan cheese,
freshly grated
1 large red apple, cored and
chopped
1 tbsp freshly squeezed lemon
juice

4 sticks celery, chopped
50g (2oz) walnuts, chopped
100g (4oz) seedless red
grapes, halved
Several coriander leaves,
roughly shredded
1 tbsp fresh parsley, chopped
Freshly ground black pepper

Dressing

150g (5oz) natural, low fat
yoghurt
2 spring onions, finely
chopped
1 clove garlic, crushed

Freshly squeezed juice of one
lemon
2 tbsp fresh parsley, chopped
Freshly ground black pepper

Arrange the mixed salad leaves on a plate. Mix the remaining salad ingredients together. Mix together the salad dressing ingredients, stir well and combine with pasta mix. Arrange pasta salad mix on salad leaves and serve immediately. Garnish with extra grated Parmesan cheese and coriander leaves.

Pesto Rice Salad (serves 4)

400g (14oz) cooked brown rice

4 tbsp fresh basil leaves, chopped

60g (2½oz) pine nuts (or walnuts), chopped

2 cloves garlic, crushed

4 tbsp freshly squeezed lemon juice

150ml (5fl oz) low fat fromage frais (or yoghurt)

60g (2½oz) Parmesan cheese, freshly grated

Pound together the garlic, nuts and basil leaves with the lemon juice, then mix with the fromage frais. Mix well with the rice and Parmesan cheese.

Crab, Olive, Sesame and Pine Nut Salad

Serves four as a starter, two as a lunch dish with crusty bread.

225g (8oz) fresh crab meat

50g (2oz) pine nuts

25g (1oz) sesame seeds

30g (1¼oz) black olives, stoned and finely chopped

225g (8oz) cold, small, new potatoes, cooked in their skins and halved

225g (8oz) mixed salad leaves

100g (4oz) watercress

Dressing

4 tbsp extra virgin olive oil

2 tbsp white wine vinegar or fresh lemon juice

1 tsp wholegrain mustard

1 spring onion, finely chopped

1 tsp acacia honey

Rock salt and freshly ground black pepper

Gently toast the pine nuts and sesame seeds until slightly coloured. Mix all the dressing ingredients in a screw-top jar, season and shake well. Toss the mixed lettuce leaves in a bowl, with a third of the dressing. Arrange the halved, new potatoes on top and coat with half the remaining dressing. Mix the remaining dressing into the crabmeat and pile on top of the potatoes. Garnish with grated Parmesan cheese and the toasted nuts and seeds. Serve immediately.

Marinaded Herring Salad (serves 8)
8 × 110g (4oz) herring fillets

Marinade

300ml (½ pt) dry white wine
4 tbsp white wine vinegar
1 tsp acacia honey
2 large spring onions, finely
   chopped

1 bay leaf
12 peppercorns (green, red
   and black mixed), crushed
2 tbsp fresh dill weed,
   chopped

Dressing

300ml (½ pt) Greek or low
   fat yoghurt
2 tbsp wholegrain mustard
2 tbsp fresh dill weed,
   chopped

1 tbsp acacia honey
1–2 tbsp freshly squeezed
   lemon juice
Rock salt and freshly ground
   black pepper

Place all the marinade ingredients in a saucepan. Cover and simmer gently for 20 minutes. Place the herring fillets in a shallow dish and pour over the boiling marinade. Cover and leave until cold. Remove the fish and skin the fillets. Chop into bite-sized chunks or leave whole if preferred. Mix the yoghurt, lemon juice, mustard dill and honey together, seasoning to taste. Pour the yoghurt mix over the herring fillets and serve chilled with salad and boiled potatoes.

This will keep for several days in the fridge.

Walnut and Coriander Pâté (serves 4)

100g (4oz) walnuts
30g (1¼oz) sesame seeds
175g (6oz) cream cheese (or
   thick fromage frais)
2 cloves garlic, crushed

1 tbsp fresh coriander leaves,
   chopped
1 tbsp walnut oil
2 tbsp semi-skimmed milk
Rock salt and freshly ground
   black pepper

Lightly toast the nuts and sesame seeds for 5 minutes under the grill. Grind the nuts and seeds until coarse. Remove half the mix and continue grinding the other half until fine. Mix together the fromage frais, garlic and coriander. Season well. Moisten the nuts with the walnut oil, then add to the fromage frais mix. Thin with a little milk if necessary. Chill before serving with wholegrain toast and watercress

Grilled Jerusalem Artichokes with Feta Cheese (serves 4)

225g (8oz) mixed lettuce leaves
4 large Jerusalem artichokes, as un-knobbly as possible
200g (7oz) Greek Feta cheese

50g (2oz) hazelnuts, crushed
1 tbsp extra virgin olive oil for basting

Dressing
4 tbsp hazelnut oil
2 tbsp fresh lemon juice
1 tsp acacia honey

Rock salt and freshly ground black pepper

Boil the artichokes until tender. Meanwhile, place all ingredients for the dressing in a screw-top jar and shake well. Season to taste. Cut the cooked artichokes in half and place upside down on a grill pan. Brush with olive oil and grill under a high heat until beginning to blacken. Turn the artichoke halves the right way up and brush the cut surfaces with olive oil. Grill until beginning to blacken. They will start to puff up and may ooze slightly. Meanwhile, toast the hazelnuts under the grill. Arrange the lettuce leaves on individual plates. Dot with Feta cheese and pour the dressing over. Add the artichoke halves and sprinkle with toasted hazelnuts. Garnish with chopped parsley.

Flashed Oysters with Lemon, Garlic and Herbs (serves 4–6)

24 oysters
100ml (4fl oz) extra virgin olive oil
100ml (4fl oz) dry white wine
1 tbsp wholegrain mustard
3 tbsp freshly squeezed lemon juice

2 cloves garlic, crushed
2 tbsp freshly chopped mixed herbs (e.g. chives, parsley, basil, coriander)
Freshly ground black pepper

Place the olive oil, white wine, garlic, mustard and herbs in a screw-top jar and shake well. If possible, leave several hours for the flavours to marinade. Open the oysters, discarding one shell. Arrange on a grill pan. Season each well with black pepper. Shake the marinade jar to emulsify the contents and spoon two teaspoons over each oyster. Flash the oysters under a hot grill for 2—3 minutes until set. Serve garnished with sprigs of watercress

Flashed Oysters with Yoghurt and Breadcrumbs (serves 4—6)

24 oysters	2 tbsp fresh parsley, chopped
300ml (10fl oz) Greek strained or low fat yoghurt	1 tbsp fresh coriander leaves, chopped
2 tbsp wholegrain mustard	A handful of fresh, wholemeal breadcrumbs
2 tbsp freshly squeezed lemon juice	Freshly ground black pepper

Mix together the yoghurt, mustard, parsley, coriander and lemon juice. Open the oysters, discarding one shell. Arrange on a grill pan. Season each well with black pepper. Spoon one tablespoon of yoghurt mixture over each oyster. Sprinkle breadcrumbs over the oysters, using as much or as little as you like. Flash under a hot grill for 2—3 minutes until set and the breadcrumbs toasted. Garnish with chopped parsley.

If you wish, a little grated cheese could be added with the breadcrumbs.

Salmon Tartare (serves 4)
This starter must be made with exceptionally fresh fish.

225g (8oz) fresh raw salmon, minced	1 tbsp fresh chives, finely chopped
2 tsp freshly squeezed lime juice	2 tbsp fresh dill weed, finely chopped
2 spring onions, finely chopped	1 tbsp wholegrain mustard
120g (4oz) low fat fromage frais	Rock salt and freshly ground black pepper

Mix together the minced salmon, lime juice and onions. Season well and mould into four flattened rounds. Mix together the fromage frais, mustard, chives and dill to make the sauce. Spoon the sauce onto a plate, carefully place the salmon round in the centre and garnish with sprigs of dill. Serve with toast and a green salad.

SOUPS

Garlic and Sesame Croutons

1 egg white
1 clove garlic, crushed
1 tbsp sesame seeds
1 tbsp soy sauce

125g (4½oz) bread, cut into 1cm (½in) cubes
8 tbsp extra virgin olive oil

Whisk together the egg white, garlic, sesame seeds and soy sauce. Dip the bread cubes in the mixture to lightly coat. Heat the olive oil until beginning to bubble. Fry the bread cubes until crispy and golden. Drain the croutons on absorbent paper.

Mediterranean Bean Soup (serves 4)

225g (8oz) dried cannellini beans
2 cloves garlic, peeled and crushed
1 large onion, peeled and coarsely chopped
2 tbsp extra virgin olive oil
1 large carrot, chopped
1 large leek, chopped
1 stick celery, chopped

1 beef tomato, chopped
1 tbsp tomato paste
1.5 litres (2½pts) vegetable/ chicken stock or water
Juice of half a lemon
1 sprig fresh rosemary
1 sprig fresh thyme
Rock salt and freshly ground black pepper

Soak the beans overnight. Change the water, and bring to the boil. Skim off any foam. Cook for ten minutes. Change the water and boil for another ten minutes. Drain. Fry the garlic and onion in olive oil until translucent. Add the remaining vegetables and fry for five minutes. Transfer vegetables, herbs, beans and water/stock to a saucepan. Cover and simmer for an hour until the beans are tender. Discard the herb sprigs and remove one ladleful of cooked vegetables. Liquidise the rest of the soup. Season with rock salt and freshly ground black pepper. Return the ladleful of vegetables to the liquidised soup along with the lemon juice and simmer gently for ten minutes. Adjust seasoning, garnish with grated Parmesan cheese and chopped herbs, and serve.

Mediterranean Fish Soup (serves 4)

1.5 litres (2½pts) water
Chopped vegetables for stock
(e.g. 1 carrot, 1 onion, 1 celery stick, 1 bay leaf, 6 crushed peppercorns, 2 cloves)
1kg (2¼lbs) mixed fish (e.g. cod, whiting, gurnard, mullet, dogfish, unpeeled prawns—don't use oily fish such as mackerel or herring)
4 tbsp extra virgin olive oil
6 cloves garlic, crushed
2 large onions, peeled and chopped
1 large leek, sliced
3 celery sticks, chopped
3 sticks Florence fennel, chopped

1 large carrot, grated
½ red pepper, deseeded and chopped
2 beef tomatoes, chopped
1 tbsp tomato paste
Juice and zest of ½ orange
2 tbsp brandy
4 tbsp dry vermouth
1 bayleaf
6 stamens saffron
2 tbsp chopped, fresh herbs (e.g. parsley, thyme, oregano, rosemary)
1 tsp finely chopped red chilli pepper *or* 1 tsp cayenne pepper
Rock salt and freshly ground black pepper

Fillet the fish and set aside the flesh for the main soup. Use the heads and bones to make the fish stock by boiling with the water and stock vegetables for 15 minutes. Strain. Sweat the onions, celery, leek, fennel and garlic in olive oil in a large saucepan until they soften and start to colour. If preferred, add more oil but this will increase the calorie count. Pour on the brandy and allow to evaporate. Add the tomatoes, tomato paste, orange juice and zest, grated carrot, red pepper, bayleaf, saffron and fish fillets. Cook until the fish flesh clouds, stirring and turning continuously. Add the strained fish stock and fresh herbs. Bring to the boil and simmer for 30 minutes. Remove the bayleaf and liquidise the soup. Season with rock salt and freshly ground black pepper and stir in the chilli pepper. Garnish with grated Parmesan, croutons and chopped fresh parsley.

Jerusalem Artichoke and Hazelnut Soup (serves 4)

450g (1lb) Jerusalem artichokes	2 tbsp hazelnut oil
Juice of 1 lemon	300ml (½pt) vegetable stock
1 medium onion, coarsely chopped	300ml (½pt) dry white wine
100g (4oz) roasted hazelnuts	Salt and freshly ground black pepper
2 tbsp extra virgin olive oil	200ml (7fl oz) Greek strained natural yoghurt

Peel and dice the artichokes. Submerge in a bowl of cold water to which the lemon juice has been added to prevent discolouring. Fry the onion in the olive oil until softened. Drain the artichokes and lightly fry in olive oil for five minutes without colouring. Pour on the vegetable stock and wine. Bring to the boil and simmer for 20 minutes. Meanwhile, crush the hazelnuts and blend with the hazelnut oil. Liquidise the soup, stir in the Greek yoghurt and season with salt and pepper to taste. Stir the hazelnut paste into the soup, reheat and adjust seasonings. Garnish with crushed, roasted hazelnuts and grated Parmesan cheese.

Mushroom, Garlic and Fennel Soup (serves 4)

450g (1lb) chestnut mush-
  rooms, chopped
3 cloves garlic, crushed
1 large onion, peeled and
  chopped
3 tbsp extra virgin olive oil
600ml (1pt) semi-skimmed
  milk

150ml (5fl oz) Greek strained
  yoghurt
24 fennel seeds, crushed
2.5cm (1in) ginger root,
  chopped
Salt and freshly ground black
  pepper

Sauté the onion and garlic in olive oil until just starting to colour. Add the mushrooms and sweat for 5 minutes. Add the milk, yoghurt, ginger and fennel seeds and bring the boil. Simmer for 20 minutes. Liquidise the soup until smooth. Season with salt and plenty of black pepper. Garnish with chopped parsley.

Alternative flavour: Substitute chopped fresh dill weed for the ginger and fennel seeds.

Lentil and Apricot Soup (serves 4)

125g (4½oz) red lentils
125g (4½oz) dried apricots
1 medium onion, chopped
2 cloves garlic, crushed
1 tbsp extra virgin olive oil
1 large potato, cubed
1 medium carrot, grated
½ red sweet pepper, finely
  chopped

300ml (½pt) dry white wine
900ml (1½pts) water
½ tsp cumin seeds, freshly
  ground
1 tsp coriander seeds, freshly
  ground
250g (9oz) low fat yoghurt

In a large saucepan, sauté the onion, garlic, cumin and coriander in olive oil until the onion starts to colour. Add all remaining ingredients except the yoghurt and bring to the boil. Cover and simmer for 30 minutes. Liquidise until smooth. Stir in the yoghurt and season to taste. Garnish with sprigs of parsley and chopped dried apricots.

SEAFOOD RECIPES

Mediterranean Herb Oil

This oil is excellent for basting fish during grilling. It takes two weeks to mature and stores well. Use within one year.

600ml (1pt) extra virgin olive oil	1 sprig tarragon
12 black peppercorns	1 sprig oregano
12 green peppercorns	2 bayleaves
12 fennel seeds	4 cloves garlic, peeled and scored
12 coriander seeds	2 red chilli peppers
1 sprig rosemary	1 tsp rock salt
1 sprig thyme	

Place all ingredients in a clear wine bottle and cork. Shake well. Leave for two weeks, if possible in a sunlit place. Shake and turn every day.

Baked Whole Fish with Lemon and Herbs (serves 4)

1.5kg (3½lb) whole round fish (e.g. sea bass, grey mullet, trout)	2 tbsp fresh parsley, chopped
	2 tbsp chopped mixed fresh herbs (e.g. fennel, dill, thyme, rosemary)
1 tbsp extra virgin olive oil (or herb-flavoured olive oil)	1 stalk lemon grass
Freshly squeezed juice of one lemon	Rock salt and freshly ground black pepper

Ask your fishmonger to gut and bone the fish and remove the head, whilst leaving the flesh whole. Trim off fins and sharp spikes. Wash the fish well, inside and out, and strip off any scales. Preheat the oven to 190°C/375°F/Gas Mark 5. Brush the fish inside and out with olive oil or home-made herb-flavoured oil. Season well. Fill the body cavity with fresh herbs and sprinkle with lemon juice. Lay the lemon grass lengthways down the centre of the fish. Season again. Wrap the fish well in silver foil and bake for 30–45 minutes.

Grilled Fish Steaks with Lemon and Herbs (serves 4)

4 × 100g (4oz) oily fish (e.g. mackerel, salmon)
1 tbsp extra virgin olive oil
4 tbsp freshly squeezed lemon juice
2 cloves garlic, crushed
4 tbsp chopped fresh herbs, (e.g. parsley, dill, rosemary, thyme)
2 spring onions, finely chopped
Freshly ground black pepper

Mix together the olive oil, lemon juice, spring onions, garlic and fresh herbs. Marinade the fish fillets in this mixture for at least one hour. Season well with black pepper. Cook under a hot grill until the flesh is just set, basting with any leftover marinade during cooking.

Bouillabaisse (serves 4–6)

1kg (2¼lb) mixed non-oily fish fillets (e.g. dogfish, John Dory, red bream, grey mullet, monkfish, cod, gurnard)
450g (1lb) mussels, cleaned and de-bearded
225g (8oz) shell-on prawns
1 large onion, chopped
3 cloves garlic, crushed
1 leek, chopped
2 beef tomatoes, chopped
1 baby bulb Florence fennel, quartered
1 sprig fennel leaf
1 sprig fresh thyme
1 sprig fresh rosemary
1 bayleaf
2 tbsp extra virgin olive oil
1200ml (2pts) water
300ml (½pt) dry white wine
Zest of one orange
1 tsp saffron
Rock salt and freshly ground black pepper

Fry the onion, leek, Florence fennel and garlic in olive oil in a large saucepan until turning golden. Add the tomatoes, saffron, thyme, fennel leaf, bayleaf and rosemary and cook for five minutes. Meanwhile, boil the water. Pour the boiling water over the vegetables and add the wine. Drop in the fish fillets, larger pieces first, and simmer for five minutes. Add the mussels and shell-on prawns and continue simmering until the mussels open. Strain the soup and place all the fish and vegetables in a large dish. Keep warm. Bring the strained liquor to the boil and whisk continuously for one minute to aid the emulsion of water and oil. When the soup has thickened, season to taste. Pour the thickened liquor over the fish. Garnish with croutons, grated Parmesan cheese and parsley, and serve with hot, crusty bread.

Mixed Seafood in Tomato, Fennel and Chilli Sauce
(serves 4)

1kg (2¼lb) fresh mussels, cleaned and de-bearded	30g (1¼oz) sun-dried tomatoes
450g (1lb) cod, haddock or monk fish or a mix of all three	250ml (9fl oz) dry white wine
100g (4oz) peeled pawns	2 tbsp extra virgin olive oil (or herb-flavoured olive oil)
1 fennel bulb, chopped	1 small red chilli pepper, deseeded and chopped
1 large onion, chopped	
2 cloves garlic, crushed	Freshly ground black pepper
1 bayleaf	Juice of half a lemon (optional)
400g (14oz) beef tomatoes, chopped	

Put the wine and mussels in a large saucepan with enough water to just cover. Add a little of the chopped onion. Bring to boil and simmer until the mussels are all opened. Remove the mussels from the pan with a slotted spoon. Continue boiling the liquor until reduced to about 100ml (¼pt). Remove the mussels from their shells. Fry the remaining chopped onion in olive oil until soft. Add the garlic and chopped fennel and fry for five minutes. Add the chilli, tomatoes and bayleaf and continue to simmer, stirring well, for 10–15 minutes. Bone and skin the fish. Cut into 2.5cm (½in) cubes. When the tomato sauce is thickened, add the fish cubes, gently pressing them down under the surface of the sauce. Cook for five minutes, or until opaque. Then add the mussels, prawns and mussel cooking liquor to the tomato fish mix. Simmer gently for 2–3 minutes. Check the seasoning and add lemon juice if necessary. Serve with fresh pasta, garnished with parsley.

Mackerel with Mustard and Herbs (serves 4)

4 × 225g (8oz) mackerel, cleaned but left whole
6 tbsp wholegrain mustard
1 tbsp fresh parsley, chopped
1 tbsp fresh chives, chopped
1 tbsp fresh lemon thyme, chopped

1 tbsp basil, chopped
Freshly squeezed juice of 1 lemon
100ml (4fl oz) dry white wine

Cut several slashes at 2.5cm (1in) intervals down each side of the mackerel. Mix together the wholegrain mustard, lemon juice and finely chopped herbs. Rub well into the cuts in the mackerel flesh. Arrange the fish in a shallow dish and pour over the white wine. Leave to marinade for at least one hour, turning occasionally. Grill the mackerel for up to 5–8 minutes per side, depending on size. Garnish with chopped parsley and serve with crusty bread and a large green salad.

Mackerel with Ginger and Fennel (serves 4)

4 × 225g (8oz) mackerel, cleaned
1 tbsp extra virgin olive oil
2 cloves garlic, crushed
1 tbsp root ginger, freshly grated

225g (8oz) onion, thinly sliced
Handful of freshly chopped fennel leaves
Freshly ground black pepper

Sauté the onion and garlic in olive oil until soft. Add the ginger and fennel. Stir-fry for one minute. Cut deep slits diagonally across each side of the mackerel, about 2.5cm (1in) apart and season with black pepper. Stuff the fish with the onion and herb mixture. Grill for 5–10 minutes per side until the flesh is cooked and sizzling. Serve with garlic bread and a green salad.

Sardines from Crete (serves 4)

4 large, fresh sardines, cleaned and scaled (about 1kg (2¼lb)
4 anchovy fillets
2 cloves garlic, crushed
1 large onion, chopped
1 courgette, chopped
1 leek, chopped
2 tbsp extra virgin olive oil
150ml (¼pt) dry white wine
225g (8oz) beef tomato, sliced
1 tbsp fresh parsley, chopped
1 tbsp fresh basil or thyme, chopped
50g (2oz) wholemeal breadcrumbs
50g (2oz) Parmesan cheese, freshly grated
Freshly ground black pepper

Fry the sardines in olive oil until nicely browned. Remove and set aside, keeping warm. Add the onion, garlic, courgette and leek to the pan and fry until softened. Pour in the wine and simmer until the liquid is reduced by half. Add the tomatoes and herbs and simmer for a further minute. Season generously with black pepper. Line an oven-proof dish with the vegetable mix and lay the sardines on top. Sprinkle with breadcrumbs and Parmesan and season further with black pepper. Flash under the grill until the cheese is browned and the breadcrumbs toasted. Decorate with anchovy fillets and serve.

Trout with Almonds (serves 4)

4 × 225g (8oz) rainbow trout
4 tbsp toasted flaked almonds
100g (4oz) Florence fennel, chopped into matchsticks
4 tbsp fresh parsley, chopped
4 tbsp freshly squeezed lemon juice
2 cloves garlic, crushed
Freshly ground black pepper

Clean the trout and remove heads, fins and tails. Using your fingers, dissect out the ribs and backbone and discard. Stuff each trout with parsley, almonds and fennel. Sprinkle with lemon juice and garlic and season well with black pepper. Cook under a hot grill until the flesh is just set *or* wrap in silver foil and bake in a hot oven (190°C/375°F/Gas Mark 5) for 20–30 minutes. Garnish with parsley.

Grilled Trout with Walnuts and Dill (serves 4)

4 × 225g (8oz) salmon trout	2 spring onions, finely
4 tbsp walnuts, chopped	chopped
8 tbsp low fat fromage frais	Freshly ground black pepper
4 tbsp fresh dill weed,	
chopped	

Clean the trout and remove heads, tails and fins. Using your fingers, dissect out the ribs and backbone and discard. Mix together the fromage frais, spring onions, walnuts and dill and stuff the cavity of each trout. Season well with freshly ground black pepper. Cook the trout under a hot grill until the flesh is just set. Garnish with lemon slices and freshly chopped dill.

Baked Orange and Rosemary Trout (serves 4)

4 × 225g (8oz) rainbow trout	A few coriander seeds,
2 medium oranges	crushed
4 sprigs fresh rosemary	Freshly ground black pepper

Preheat the oven to 190°C/375°F/Gas Mark 5. Clean the trout and remove heads, fins and tails. Using your fingers, dissect out the ribs and backbone and discard. Peel the oranges and slice the flesh. Stuff the trout with sliced orange, rosemary sprigs and the coriander seeds. Season well with freshly ground black pepper. Wrap in silver foil and bake for 20 minutes. Garnish with coriander leaves.

Salmon in Dill Sauce (serves 4)

4 × 120g (4oz) salmon fillets
150g (5oz) low fat fromage
  frais
2 tbsp freshly squeezed lemon
  juice

4 tbsp fresh dill weed,
  chopped
Freshly ground black pepper

Preheat the oven to 190°C/375°F/Gas Mark 5. Mix together the fromage frais, lemon juice and dill to make the sauce. Place the salmon fillets on a sheet of silver foil. Top the fish with dill sauce and season well. Wrap up the fish in silver foil to make a parcel (make four individual parcels if you wish). Bake for 15–20 minutes. Garnish with lemon wedges and fresh dill leaves

Sea Bass with Fennel (serves 4–6)

1 kg (2¼lbs) sea bass (scaled,
  gutted and with head
  removed)
1 tbsp extra virgin olive oil
  (or herb-flavoured olive
  oil)
4 baby bulbs Florence fennel

50g (2oz) fresh fennel leaves,
  finely chopped
300ml (½pt) fish stock
1 tbsp Pernod or pastis
Rock salt and freshly ground
  black pepper

Pre-heat the oven to 200°C/400°F/Gas Mark 6. Rub the bass well with salt and black pepper. Cut slits at 2.5cm (1in) intervals across the skin on each side. Blanch the fennel bulbs in boiling water for one minute. Cut into quarters. Slide slices of fennel into each slit in the bass. Brush both sides of the fish with olive oil. Stuff the cavity with chopped fennel leaves. Lay the sea bass in an oven-proof dish. Arrange any remaining pieces of fennel bulb around it. Pour over the fish stock and Pernod. Cook in a hot oven for 20 minutes.

White Fish with Walnut Sauce (serves 4)

1.5kg (3½lb) whole white
fish, cleaned
100g (4oz) fresh walnuts
1 slice crustless white bread
soaked in milk

2 tbsp extra virgin olive oil
1 tbsp freshly squeezed lemon
juice
1 tbsp fresh coriander leaves,
chopped

Court Bouillon
1 sprig fresh thyme
1 bayleaf
1 litre (1¾pts) or more water
to cover fish

4 peppercorns
1 stalk celery
1 carrot, grated
1 large onion, sliced

Bring the ingredients for the court bouillon to the boil. Add the fish and poach gently for 30 minutes. Remove and leave to drain. Pound together the walnuts, bread, olive oil, lemon juice and coriander leaves until the sauce is the consistency of paste. Add a little more milk if necessary. Arrange the fish on a plate. Spoon over the walnut sauce and garnish with sprigs of coriander and lemon wedges. Eat hot or cold.

Moules Marinières

Serve four as a main course or six as a starter

2kg (4½lb) fresh mussels,
cleaned
1 medium onion, finely
chopped
3 cloves garlic, crushed
4 tbsp fresh parsley, chopped

2 tbsp extra virgin olive oil
1 bottle dry white wine
1 sprig fresh thyme and 1
stem fresh tarragon or
rosemary tied together
Freshly ground black pepper

Fry the onion and garlic in a saucepan until soft. Add the wine, bouquet garni and parsley. Bring to the boil and simmer for two minutes. Add the cleaned mussels and plenty of freshly ground black pepper. Cover and simmer for 8–10 minutes, or until all the mussels have opened. Don't overcook or the mussels will shrivel and become rubbery. They should remain plump with their flesh just set. Remove the bouquet garni and garnish with freshly chopped parsley. Serve immediately with hot, crusty bread.

Mussels Stuffed with Coriander, Walnuts and Cheese
(serves 4–6)

48 large mussels
60ml (2fl oz) dry white wine
120ml (4fl oz) walnut oil
100g (4oz) walnuts, crushed
2 cloves garlic, crushed

4 tbsp fresh coriander leaves, chopped
50g (2oz) Parmesan cheese, freshly grated
30g (1¼oz) dried breadcrumbs
Freshly ground black pepper

Place the cleaned mussels and white wine in a covered saucepan and steam over a strong heat for five minutes. Shake the pan frequently until all mussels are opened. Strain, reserving the liquor as stock for another recipe. When the mussels are cool enough to handle, discard the empty top shell and any remaining beards. Mix together the crushed garlic, crushed walnuts, coriander leaves and walnut oil. Season well with freshly ground black pepper. Arrange the half mussel shells on a grilling pan. Divide the walnut mixture between them. Mix together the breadcrumbs and Parmesan cheese and sprinkle over each shell. When ready to serve, flash under the grill.

MEAT DISHES

Tarragon Chicken (serves 4)

4 chicken pieces, de-skinned and boned
1 tbsp extra virgin olive oil
1 onion, finely chopped
1 clove garlic, crushed
1 tbsp flour
150ml (¼pt) white wine

300ml (½pt) water/chicken stock (made from the bones, without the skin)
Handful of fresh tarragon leaves, de-stalked and finely chopped
Rock salt and freshly ground black pepper

Sauté the chicken pieces in oil until beginning to colour. Remove and keep warm. Fry the chopped onion and garlic until softened. Sprinkle over the flour and cook, stirring until all the oil is absorbed. Slowly add the wine and chicken stock, and bring to the boil, stirring continuously so that no lumps form. Add the tarragon leaves. Simmer to reduce slightly, then season to taste. Return the chicken pieces to the pan. Cover and cook gently for 20 minutes. Garnish with tarragon leaves.

Spicy Chicken with Lemon and Olives (serves 4)

4 chicken breasts, de-skinned and boned
1 clove garlic, crushed
1 tsp fresh ginger root, chopped
1 red chilli pepper, finely chopped (de-seed if you wish to reduce heat)
¼ tsp cumin seed, freshly ground
½ tsp coriander seeds, freshly ground
2 tbsp extra virgin olive oil
200ml (7fl oz) chicken stock/ water

100ml (4fl oz) dry white wine
1 onion, finely chopped
3 tbsp fresh parsley, chopped
3 tbsp fresh coriander leaves, chopped
Pinch of saffron (or ½ tsp turmeric root, powdered)
30g (1¼oz) green olives, stoned and halved
1 lemon, sliced
Rock salt and freshly ground black pepper

Mix together the olive oil, garlic, ginger, chilli, cumin and coriander seeds. Rub well into the chicken breasts. Place the chicken pieces in an earthenware dish. Cover and marinade overnight in the fridge.

When ready to cook, place the chicken pieces, onion, parsley, coriander leaves and saffron (or turmeric) in a saucepan. Pour on the water and wine and bring to the boil. Simmer gently for 20 minutes. Add the olives and lemon slices. Cook gently for a further 10 minutes. Remove the chicken pieces, lemons and olives with a slotted spoon. Place in a serving dish and keep warm. Reduce the sauce and season to taste. Pour the sauce over the chicken and serve with couscous or rice.

Orange Chicken with Walnuts and Herbs (serves 6)

2 tbsp extra virgin olive oil
1.5kg (3½lb) boiling chicken, skinned
1 large onion, chopped
2 cloves garlic, crushed
300ml (½pt) chicken or vegetable stock
120ml (4fl oz) dry white wine
100g (4oz) chopped walnuts
1 bunch fresh parsley, chopped
1 bunch fresh chives, chopped
6 tbsp fresh coriander leaves, chopped
4 tbsp mint, freshly chopped
175ml (6fl oz) freshly squeezed orange juice plus grated zest of two oranges
Rock salt and freshly ground black pepper

In a large pan, sweat the onion and garlic in olive oil until soft. Add the chicken, wine and stock and season well with black pepper. Bring to the boil, cover and simmer for one hour. Add the chopped walnuts, fresh herbs, orange juice and rind. Continue simmering for a further 30 minutes. Garnish with walnut halves. Serve with salad and brown rice.

Roast Rosemary Lamb with Cannellini Beans (serves 6)

225g (8oz) dried cannellini beans, soaked overnight
Water to just cover the soaked beans
1 bouquet garni (1 bayleaf, 1 sprig rosemary, 1 sprig thyme, tied together)
6 juniper berries
6 peppercorns
2 cloves garlic, crushed
1 onion
1 beef tomato, chopped
1 tbsp tomato purée
2 tbsp fresh parsley, chopped
1 tbsp fresh sage (or thyme), chopped
1 tbsp fresh coriander leaves, chopped

Lamb
1kg (2¼lb) lamb, lean fillet of leg, boned
4 cloves garlic, sliced
4–6 sprigs of fresh rosemary
3 tbsp extra virgin olive oil
Rock salt and freshly ground black pepper

Cover the soaked cannellini beans with water, add the bouquet garni, juniper berries, peppercorns and crushed garlic. Bring to the boil and simmer for 1¼ hours whilst preparing the meat. Top up with water as necessary to prevent boiling dry.

Meanwhile heat the over to 180°C/350°F/Gas Mark 4. With a skewer make holes from one end of the lamb joint to the other. Using the skewer, thread the rosemary sprigs through the centre of the meat. Make little pockets all over the meat with a sharp knife and insert slices of garlic. Brush the joint with extra virgin olive oil. Season well with salt and pepper.

After the beans have been cooking for 1¼ hours, place the lamb joint in the oven and roast for 45 minutes, basting occasionally with olive oil.

Add the onion, chopped tomato and purée to the beans. Continue cooking until the meat is ready, allowing the bean mixture to boil fairly dry at the end—without burning. Then drain the beans and discard the bouquet garni. Stir in the chopped herbs and season well. Place the lamb joint in the middle of a serving plate and surround with the beans. Garnish with sprigs of rosemary.

Lamb Lasagne (serves 4)

450g (1lb) lean minced lamb	2 tbsp fresh parsley, chopped
1 tbsp extra virgin olive oil	150ml (½pt) light red wine
400g (14oz) fresh tomatoes, all chopped except one	150ml (½pt) water
	12 sheets easy-cook spinach lasagne
25g (1oz) sun-dried tomato (optional)	250g (9oz) low fat natural yoghurt
2 tbsp tomato purée	
2 cloves garlic, crushed	60g (2½oz) Parmesan cheese, freshly grated
1 large onion, chopped	
1 carrot, grated	Rock salt and freshly ground black pepper
1 tsp fresh rosemary, chopped	

Fry the onion and garlic in the oil for 5 minutes. Add the minced lamb and fry for a further 5 minutes. Add the grated carrot, the chopped tomatoes (including sun-dried if used), tomato purée, wine, water and herbs. Cover and simmer for 30 minutes, stirring occasionally.

Preheat the oven to 180°C/350°F/Gas Mark 4. Brush an ovenproof dish with olive oil and line the base with four sheets of oven-ready lasagne. Top with half the lamb sauce, then spread with one third of the yoghurt. Repeat the pasta, meat and yoghurt layers and top with remaining pasta and yoghurt. Thinly slice the remaining whole tomato. Decorate the top of the lasagne with tomato slices then sprinkle with Parmesan cheese. Bake for 45 minutes.

Mediterranean Moussaka (serves 4)

350g (12oz) lean, minced lamb	2 tbsp tomato purée *or* 2 sun-dried tomatoes, chopped
1 tbsp extra virgin olive oil	75ml (2½fl oz) red wine
1 onion, chopped	1 tbsp fresh parsley, chopped
1 leek, chopped	1 small sprig fresh rosemary
2 cloves garlic, crushed	1 bayleaf
1 small carrot, grated	1 medium aubergine, sliced
½ small Florence fennel bulb, chopped	120g (4oz) potatoes, sliced
225g (8oz) tomatoes, chopped	Rock salt and freshly ground black pepper

For the sauce

300ml (10fl oz) low fat yoghurt	¼ tsp nutmeg, freshly ground
2 tsp cornflour	1 tbsp fresh parsley, chopped
2 size 4 eggs, lightly whisked	Freshly ground black pepper

Topping
60g (2½oz) Parmesan cheese, freshly grated

Heat the oven to 180°C/350°F/Gas Mark 4. Fry the onion, leek and garlic until beginning to colour. Add the minced lamb and fry for 5 minutes. Season well. Bring a pan of water to the boil and add the sliced potato. Cook for five minutes. Drain excess fat from the lamb. Then add the tomatoes, tomato purée, carrot, fennel, red wine and herbs. Simmer for 15 minutes. Add the sliced aubergine to the potatoes and continue boiling for a further 5 minutes.

Blend the cornflour and yoghurt together, add the remaining sauce ingredients and lightly whisk. Season to taste.

Place a thin layer of potato and aubergine in the base of an oven-proof casserole dish. Top with the lamb mixture and repeat, finishing with a layer of potato and aubergine. Press down well. Pour the sauce on top, drizzle with grated Parmesan and ground black pepper and bake for 30 minutes, or until the topping is golden.

Lamb Curry (serves 4)

1kg (2¼lb) joint lamb, boned and cubed	2.5cm (1in) ginger root, finely chopped
225g (8oz) Greek strained yoghurt	600ml (1pt) water
1 large onion, sliced	1 tbsp ground amchoor (mango) powder
4 cloves garlic	450g (1lb) mixed, chopped
2 beef tomatoes, chopped	vegetables (e.g. potatoes,
2 tbsp extra virgin olive oil	okra, spinach, chickpeas)
1–4 chilli peppers, chopped (depending on desired heat)	1 large bunch of fresh coriander leaves, chopped

The curry powder

Coarsely grind together the following:	6 green cardamoms
	2 cloves
1 tbsp coriander seed	2.5cm (1in) cinnamon bark
1 tsp cumin seed	1 tsp powdered turmeric
1 tsp fenugreek	1 bayleaf
1 tsp mustard seed	1 tsp rock salt

Mix together the freshly ground curry powder and the Greek yoghurt. Pour onto the lamb and marinade for at least 4 hours, if not overnight. Fry the onion and garlic in olive oil until starting to colour. Add the curried lamb and yoghurt mix and cook, stirring gently, for ten minutes. Add the chopped ginger root, chilli, tomatoes, additional vegetables (if used) and enough water to just cover. Cover and simmer gently for 30 minutes. Add the amchoor powder and chopped coriander leaf and cook for a further 10 minutes, reducing the liquid to the consistency of a thick sauce. Garnish with fresh coriander leaves.

VEGETARIAN DISHES

Green Herbed Omelette (serves 4)

6–8 eggs, depending on size	1 tbsp fresh coriander leaves, chopped
1 tbsp extra virgin olive oil	
1 leek, chopped	1 tbsp fresh basil, chopped
4 spring onions, chopped	1 tbsp walnuts, chopped
100g (4oz) spinach, freshly chopped	2 tbsp Parmesan cheese, freshly grated
2 tbsp fresh parsley, chopped	Rock salt and freshly ground black pepper
1 tbsp fresh tarragon, chopped	

Preheat the oven to 180°C/350°F/Gas Mark 4. Beat the eggs together in a large bowl and add the chopped vegetables, herbs and walnuts. Season well. Oil an ovenproof dish and pour in the mixture. Sprinkle with Parmesan cheese. Cover and bake for 20 minutes. Then uncover and brown for a further 15 minutes until the top is golden. Serve with crusty bread and a green salad.

Ratatouille (serves 4)

1 large onion, sliced	150ml (¼pt) white wine
2 cloves garlic, crushed	1 tbsp fresh parsley, chopped
1 tbsp coriander seeds, crushed	1 tbsp fresh basil, chopped
1 large sweet red pepper, deseeded and sliced lengthways	1 tbsp fresh coriander leaves, chopped
1 large aubergine, chopped	1 tsp fresh thyme, chopped
1 large courgette, chopped	1 tbsp extra virgin olive oil
4 beef tomatoes, chopped	Rock salt and freshly ground black pepper

Using a large saucepan, sweat the onion and garlic in olive oil until translucent. Add the red pepper, coriander seed and aubergines and stir-fry for five minutes. Add all the remaining ingredients, cover and simmer with the lid on for 30 minutes. Stir occasionally. Season to taste with salt and black pepper, then serve immediately.

Roasted Red Pepper Devils (serves 4)

4 large red peppers
2 beef tomatoes, cut into eighths
2 cloves garlic, crushed
2 tbsp extra virgin olive oil
2 tbsp walnut oil
Freshly squeezed juice of one lemon
2 tbsp fresh basil, chopped
2 tbsp fresh coriander leaves, chopped
16 anchovy fillets
2 tbsp capers
1 red chilli pepper, finely chopped
Cayenne pepper
Freshly ground black pepper

Preheat oven to 180°C/350°F/Gas Mark 4. Cut the red peppers and stalks in half, lengthways, and remove seeds. Combine the olive and walnut oils and use to lightly brush each pepper inside and out. Place peppers on a baking sheet or in a shallow tray. Place the crushed garlic and half the chopped basil and coriander leaves inside the pepper halves. Season with black pepper. Place two pieces of beef tomato inside each pepper half. Divide the anchovies, capers and chilli pepper between the pepper halves and sprinkle with cayenne pepper. Curl an anchovy fillet round each piece of tomato. Place the peppers in the oven and roast for 45–50 minutes, until the skins have started to char. Garnish with the remaining basil and coriander leaves.

Aubergines Parmesan (serves 4)

2 large aubergines, sliced
  lengthways
4 tbsp extra virgin olive oil
1 large onion, sliced
4 cloves garlic, crushed
700g (1¾lb) beef tomatoes
2 tbsp tomato purée

120ml (4fl oz) dry white wine
2 tbsp fresh basil, chopped
1 tbsp fresh oregano, chopped
1 tbsp fresh parsley, chopped
225g (8oz) mozzarella, sliced,
  or low-fat Cheddar cheese,
  grated

Topping
60g (2½oz) freshly grated Parmesan cheese

1 beef tomato, sliced
Garnish: freshly chopped basil

Preheat oven to 180°C/350°F/Gas Mark 4. Fry the onion and garlic in 1 tbsp olive oil for 5 minutes until beginning to colour. Add the tomatoes, tomato purée, white wine and chopped herbs. Cover and simmer for 30 minutes, stirring occasionally. Season to taste.

Brush the pan with some of the remaining olive oil and lightly fry the aubergine slices in batches until soft and beginning to colour. Re-brush the pan between batches, trying to keep the absorption of oil to a minimum. Drain the aubergine slices on absorbent paper.

Layer the tomato sauce, aubergine slices and mozzarella cheese in a casserole dish, starting and finishing with tomato sauce. Top with a layer of sliced beef tomato and sprinkle with Parmesan cheese. Bake for 30 minutes or until nicely browned. Serve garnished with chopped basil.

Stuffed Cinnamon Aubergines (serves 4)

2 large aubergines
1 tbsp pine kernels (or
  chopped walnuts)
3 tbsp extra virgin olive oil
2 large onions
2 cloves garlic
2 beef tomatoes, chopped
½ tsp cinnamon, freshly ground

½ tsp coriander seed, freshly
  ground
½ tsp acacia honey
1 tbsp fresh parsley, chopped
1 tbsp fresh coriander leaf,
  chopped
Rock salt and freshly ground
  black pepper

Preheat the oven to 180°C/350°F/Gas Mark 4. Cut the leaf base from the aubergines, cover with boiling water and boil for 10 minutes. Drain, then plunge into cold water until cool enough to handle. Cut the aubergines in half, lengthways. Scoop out most of the flesh, leaving a 1cm (½in) thick shell. Lightly oil the insides of the hollowed shells and season well. Place on a greased oven tray and bake for 30 minutes. Meanwhile, chop the scooped out flesh.

Fry the onions and garlic in 1 tbsp olive oil for five minutes or until beginning to colour. Add the chopped tomatoes, honey, herbs and spices. Simmer for 15 minutes. Add the chopped aubergine flesh and pine kernels to the mixture and continue cooking for 10 minutes. Season to taste.

Remove the aubergine shells from the oven. Stuff them with the spiced tomato and aubergine mixture and serve immediately.

Aubergine and Spinach with Basil and Walnuts (serves 4)

450g (1lb) aubergines, sliced lengthways
2 tbsp extra virgin olive oil
450g (1lb) baby spinach leaves, chopped

120g (4oz) mozzarella (or Cheddar) cheese, grated
30g (1¼oz) Parmesan, freshly grated

Sauce
1 tbsp extra virgin olive oil
1 onion, chopped
2 cloves garlic, crushed
450g (1lb) beef tomatoes, chopped
1 red pepper, deseeded and cut into strips
1 tbsp tomato purée
1 tbsp fresh basil, chopped

1 tbsp fresh oregano, chopped
1 tbsp fresh parsley, chopped
100g (4oz) mushrooms, sliced
100g (4oz) walnuts, coarsely chopped
100ml (4fl oz) dry white wine
Rock salt and freshly ground black pepper

Lightly brush a heavy pan with olive oil and fry the long aubergine slices until starting to colour. Drain on absorbent paper. Place the spinach leaves in a saucepan with a few tablespoons water. Cover and steam until tender. Preheat the oven to 190°C/375°F/Gas Mark 5.

Sauce

Purée the tomatoes in a blender. Fry the onion and garlic until beginning to colour. Add the blended tomatoes, tomato purée, herbs and white wine. Bring to the boil and cook, stirring, until starting to thicken. Add the red pepper and mushrooms and simmer for five minutes. Add a little water or more wine if the sauce becomes too thick. Remove from heat and season. Stir in the walnuts. Place alternating layers of aubergine slices, sauce and spinach in an oven-proof dish. Top with the grated cheese and bake for 30 minutes. Serve with pasta or hot, crusty bread and salad.

Cheese and Lentil Herb Loaf (serves 4)

175g (6oz) red lentils	1 tbsp freshly squeezed lemon
350ml (12fl oz) water	juice
100g (4oz) grated low fat	1 egg size 1
hard cheese (e.g. reduced-	3 tbsp Greek strained natural
fat cheddar)	yoghurt
1 onion, chopped	1 tbsp tomato purée
2 tbsp walnuts, chopped	2 beef tomatoes, thinly sliced
1 tbsp fresh parsley, chopped	Salt and freshly ground black
1 tbsp fresh chives, chopped	pepper
1 tbsp fresh basil, chopped	A little olive oil
½ tsp cayenne pepper	

Preheat the oven to 190°C/375°F/Gas Mark 5. Rinse the lentils. Place in a tightly covered pan with the water. Simmer for 10–15 minutes. The lentils should reduce to a stiff purée. Moisten with a little more water if necessary. Remove from the heat and mix in the grated low fat cheese, walnuts, onion, chopped herbs and cayenne pepper. Beat the egg lightly and stir in the yoghurt, lemon juice and tomato purée. Add the egg mixture to the lentil mix and combine thoroughly.

Brush the inside of a 450g (1lb) loaf tin with olive oil. Line with one third of the sliced tomatoes. Add one third of the lentil mixture and press down well. Top with half the remaining beef tomato slices. Add half the remaining lentil mix and press down well. Top with the remaining tomato slices. Finally, add the remaining lentil mix and press down. Bake for 45–50 minutes until the top is golden brown. Leave to stand in the tin for 10 minutes before turning out.

Walnut and Mushroom Nut Roast (serves 6)

1 tbsp extra virgin olive oil	1 tsp yeast extract (if not
1 onion, finely chopped	using stock)
2 cloves garlic	8 long asparagus stalks,
225g (8oz) walnuts, ground	lightly steamed
120g (4oz) fresh wholemeal	½ sweet red pepper, cut into
breadcrumbs	strips lengthways
1 egg, size 1	120g (4oz) chestnut or brown
3 medium parsnips, boiled	cap mushrooms, chopped
3 tbsp Greek strained yoghurt	Rock salt and freshly ground
1 tsp fresh rosemary, chopped	black pepper
1 tsp fresh thyme, chopped	Garnish: 4 walnut halves; 2
1 tbsp fresh parsley, chopped	small bayleaves
150ml (¼pt) hot water or stock	Olive oil for greasing loaf tin

Preheat the oven to 180°C/350°F/Gas Mark 4. Fry the onion, mushrooms and garlic until beginning to brown. Mash the parsnips together with the yoghurt and fresh herbs. Season well. Beat the egg and add to the ground walnuts and breadcrumbs. Fold into the parsnip mix with the fried onion, mushrooms and garlic. Add the stock or yeast extract dissolved in hot water to the nut roast mix. Combine well and season to taste.

Lightly brush a 900g (2lb) loaf tin with olive oil. Arrange the four walnut halves and 2 bayleaves in the base, so they form a pattern when the loaf is turned out. Layer a third of the nut roast mix in the bottom of the loaf tin. Arrange half the red pepper strips and asparagus stalks lengthways on top. Add half the remaining mix and top with the remaining pepper strips and asparagus. Finally, top with the remaining nut roast mix.

Cover with foil and bake for 50 minutes. Leave to stand for 10 minutes before turning out.

Mediterranean Fennel Bake (serves 4)

450g (1lb) Florence fennel bulbs, thinly sliced
1 tbsp extra virgin olive oil
1 large onion, chopped
3 cloves garlic, crushed
3 beef tomatoes, sliced
1 tbsp fresh parsley, chopped
1 tbsp fresh basil, chopped
1 glass red wine
Rock salt and freshly ground black pepper
50g (2oz) fresh wholemeal breadcrumbs
50g (2oz) Parmesan cheese, freshly grated

Fry the onion and garlic until beginning to colour. Add the sliced fennel and stir-fry for five minutes. Add the tomatoes, red wine, and chopped herbs. Cover and simmer gently for thirty minutes. Add seasoning. Pour into an earthenware serving dish. Top with the breadcrumbs and grated Parmesan cheese. Grill until crisp and golden. Serve immediately.

Mediterranean Chickpeas (serves 4)

225g (8oz) chickpeas, soaked overnight
2 tbsp extra virgin olive oil
1 onion, chopped
3 cloves garlic, crushed
450g (1lb) beef tomatoes, chopped
225g (8oz) spinach, chopped
1 tsp cumin seeds, freshly ground
1 tbsp coriander seeds, freshly ground
2 tbsp fresh coriander leaves, chopped
1 tbsp fresh parsley, chopped
1 tbsp fresh oregano, chopped
100g (4oz) mozzarella (or low fat Cheddar) grated
60g (2½oz) Parmesan, freshly grated
4 tbsp Greek strained yoghurt

Simmer the soaked chickpeas in water for 45 minutes until tender. Drain, reserving the cooking liquor. Liquidise one quarter of the chickpeas with a little liquor to make a smooth paste. Fry the onion and garlic in olive oil until beginning to colour. Add the ground seeds and the remaining whole chickpeas. Cook, stirring for five minutes. Stir in the chopped spinach, tomatoes and herbs. Add 200ml (7fl oz) cooking liquor and bring to the boil. Simmer for five minutes. Remove from the heat. Season to taste. Add the grated cheese and yoghurt and stir until the cheese has melted.

PASTA

Pasta is ready to eat when it is *al dente*, which means it is sticky to the teeth. The traditional way of checking this with spaghetti is to throw a strand at a wall. If it sticks, the pasta is ready to eat. When draining pasta, leave a little water clinging to the strands. This helps a sauce to coat the pasta more easily.

Pasta with Pesto (serves 4)

450g (1lb) fresh spinach tagliatelle (or 350g (13oz) dried pasta)
2 cloves garlic, crushed
2 tbsp nuts, lightly toasted
50g (2oz) fresh basil leaves
50ml (2fl oz) extra virgin olive oil
50ml (2fl oz) walnut oil (or more olive oil)
60g (2½oz) Parmesan, freshly grated
Rock salt and freshly ground black pepper

Blend or pound the oil, nuts, garlic and basil into a smooth paste. Stir in the cheese. Season to taste. Meanwhile, cook the pasta in plenty of boiling water until *al dente*. Drain but leave moist so the sauce will coat the pasta well. Add the pasta to the pesto sauce. Toss well and serve with a green salad.

Pasta with Walnuts and Coriander (serves 4)

450g (1lb) fresh spinach pasta (or 350g (13oz) dried pasta)
50g (2oz) walnuts, crushed
2 cloves garlic, crushed
1 tsp coriander seed, crushed
2 tbsp fresh coriander leaves, chopped
1 tbsp fresh parsley, chopped
1 tsp fresh oregano/marjoram, chopped
50ml (2fl oz) walnut oil
25ml (1fl oz) extra virgin olive oil
60g (2½oz) Parmesan, freshly grated
Rock salt and freshly ground black pepper

Blend or pound the oil, nuts, garlic, herbs and seeds into a smooth paste. Stir in the cheese. Season to taste. Meanwhile, cook the pasta in plenty of boiling water until *al dente*. Drain but leave moist so the sauce will coat the pasta well. Add the pasta to the coriander walnut sauce. Toss well and serve with a green salad.

Pasta with Fennel and Mixed Mediterranean Herbs (serves 4)

450g (1lb) fresh spinach pasta (or 350g (13oz) dried pasta)
1 onion, finely chopped
2 cloves garlic, crushed
4 tbsp extra virgin olive oil
1 small bulb Florence fennel, chopped into matchsticks
1 tbsp fresh parsley, chopped
1 tbsp fresh basil, chopped
1 tbsp fresh oregano/ marjoram, chopped
1 tbsp fresh thyme, chopped
1 tsp fresh rosemary, chopped
Rock salt and freshly ground black pepper

Sauté the onion, fennel and garlic in olive oil until beginning to colour. Meanwhile, cook the pasta in plenty of boiling water until *al dente*. Drain but leave moist so the sauce will coat the pasta well. Add the freshly chopped herbs and pasta to the fennel mixture and stir-fry for one minute. Season to taste.

Pasta with Tomato and Mozzarella Sauce (serves 4)

450g (1lb) fresh spinach pasta (or 350g (13oz) dried pasta)
4 tbsp extra virgin olive oil
1 onion, chopped
2 cloves garlic, crushed
450g (1lb) beef tomatoes, skinned and chopped
50ml (½ glass) dry white wine
100g (4oz) mozzarella cheese, grated
60g (2½oz) Parmesan, grated
1 tbsp fresh oregano/ marjoram, chopped
Freshly ground black pepper

Sauté the onion and garlic in olive oil until beginning to colour. Add the tomatoes, oregano and wine and cook, stirring occasionally, for 15 minutes. Meanwhile, cook the pasta in plenty of boiling water until *al dente*. Drain but leave moist so the sauce will coat the pasta well. Add the pasta to the sauce. Mix and season well. Top with the cheese and flash under the grill until the cheese is melted.

Pasta with Smoked Salmon and Fennel (serves 4)

450g (1lb) fresh spinach or wholemeal pasta (or 350g (13oz) dried pasta)
1 small bulb Florence fennel, chopped into matchsticks
2 cloves garlic, crushed
1 tbsp extra virgin olive oil
1 tbsp freshly squeezed lemon juice
Zest of half a lemon
1 tbsp fennel leaves, chopped
300ml (10fl oz) low fat fromage frais or yoghurt
175g (6oz) smoked salmon, cut into thin strips
Rock salt and freshly ground black pepper

Sauté the garlic and Florence fennel in the oil until beginning to colour. Season well. Add the fennel leaves, lemon juice, zest and fromage frais or yoghurt. Heat through, stirring continuously. Do not allow to boil or the yoghurt may clot. Meanwhile, cook the pasta in plenty of water until *al dente*. Drain but leave moist so the sauce will coat the pasta well. Combine the pasta and fennel sauce. Toss well then add the smoked salmon strips. Garnish with fennel leaves and serve immediately with crusty bread and salad.

Pasta with Tomato, Tuna and Basil Sauce (serves 4)

450g (1lb) fresh spinach or wholemeal pasta (or 350g (13oz) dried pasta)
2 tbsp extra virgin olive oil
1 onion, chopped
2 cloves garlic, crushed
350g (13oz) beef tomatoes, chopped
50ml (2fl oz) dry white wine

200g (7oz) tuna fish, flaked
12 black olives, stoned and chopped
1 tbsp wholegrain mustard
1 chilli, fresh or dried, chopped
1 tbsp fresh parsley, chopped
Freshly ground black pepper

Sauté the onion and garlic in olive oil until beginning to colour. Add the chopped tomatoes, chilli and wine and simmer gently for 10 minutes, stirring occasionally. Add the tuna fish, mustard, olives and parsley and simmer gently for 10 minutes. Season well. Meanwhile, cook the pasta in plenty of boiling water until *al dente*. Drain but leave slightly moist so the sauce will coat the pasta well. Toss the pasta and sauce together and garnish with parsley and grated Parmesan cheese.

CHAPTER 9

Prevention and Treatment with Drugs

HRT

For women who are able and happy to take hormone replacement therapy (HRT), it can help to prevent, or at least postpone, osteoporosis.

What is HRT?

Hormone replacement therapy (HRT) is a way of giving you back the natural level of the oestrogen hormone that your ovaries stop making at the menopause. It can be used to:

- relieve menopausal symptoms such as hot flushes, night sweats and mood swings;
- prevent a premature menopause in women whose ovaries are removed;
- treat vaginal dryness or stress incontinence;
- reduce your lifetime risk of coronary heart disease;
- reduce your lifetime risk of osteoporosis;
- reduce your risk of future senile dementia.

The only hormone replacement that is thought to be needed is oestrogen. Oestrogen cannot be given on its own, however, if you still have an intact uterus. This is because oestrogen alone overstimulates the womb lining, which may prove harmful over a prolonged period of time. Natural progesterone cannot be given by mouth as it is broken down in the stomach. A synthetic version (known as a progestogen) is therefore given along with the oestrogen to protect the womb lining.

How does HRT act on bones to prevent osteoporosis?
Osteoporosis develops when the activity of bone-building cells (osteoblasts) and bone-absorbing cells (osteoclasts) becomes unbalanced so that too little new bone is made to replace that which is reabsorbed. Oestrogen is important for maintaining the balance—it stimulates activity of osteoblasts and has other beneficial effects on calcium metabolism that increase the amount of calcium deposited in bone. Once oestrogen levels fall after the menopause, the risk of osteoporosis therefore starts to increase.

Women who have a low bone mass at the time of the menopause (e.g. through poor diet, too little exercise) have twice the risk of an osteoporotic fracture once their oestrogen levels fall. Some women also inherit the tendency to lose bone more quickly than usual after the menopause, so their risk of a bone fracture is trebled once oestrogen levels fall.

By taking HRT after the menopause, a healthy bone balance is maintained and bone thinning is postponed. Once oestrogen replacement stops, however, the imbalance will recur and bone thinning will resume.

How effective is HRT in preventing osteoporosis?
Oestrogen replacement therapy reduces the risk of a woman developing a hip fracture after the menopause by 10–40 per cent after seven or more years of use. This compares with other preventative treatments as follows:

- oestrogen reduces the risk of vertebral fracture by 40 per cent;
- the drug etidronate reduces the risk of vertebral fracture by 40 per cent;

- calcium supplements reduce the risk of vertebral fracture by 20 per cent;
- calcium and vitamin D reduce the risk of non-vertebral and hip fracture by 30–40 per cent.

Oestrogen seems to reduce the risk of osteoporosis more than expected from its effects on bone density. It is thought to increase bone quality, making it stronger as well as maintaining its mass.

Unfortunately, bone loss continues once oestrogen replacement stops. One study suggests that protection against fractures is lost within five years of coming off treatment. Hormone replacement therapy effectively buys your bones time. This means that bone thinning below the level linked with an increased risk of fracture is less likely to occur during your natural lifespan.

What are the other health benefits of HRT?
Taking oestrogen replacement therapy can also:

- improve menopausal symptoms such as hot flushes, night sweats and emotional symptoms;
- improve vaginal dryness, bladder problems and low sex drive;
- reduce your risk of coronary heart disease after the menopause by up to 50 per cent;
- reduce the risk of a second heart attack (in women who have already had one) by 80 per cent;
- decrease your risk of dementia or Alzheimer's disease by up to 50 per cent after seven years.

What HRT preparations are available?
HRT is available as:

traditional tablets	vaginal creams
skin patches	vaginal pessaries
skin gels	vaginal rings
implants	

An intra-uterine progestogen coil, used together with oral oes-trogen tablets, is currently under trial.

Will HRT mean my periods return?
If you have not had a hysterectomy, taking HRT does not inevitably mean you will restart your periods:

- One synthetic hormone, tibolone, has both oestrogen and progesterone effects in the body. This means it can control oestrogen withdrawal symptoms and protect the womb lining from overstimulation without the need for a separate progestogen. In nine out of ten cases it does not trigger the return of a withdrawal bleed so long as you have not had a natural period for at least one year.
- Some formulations of HRT provide continuous hormone therapy without triggering a regular monthly bleed.
- One formulation provides a 70-day course of hormones, so that you only have a withdrawal bleed once every three months.

How long should I take HRT?
Current medical advice is that where HRT is indicated, it should ideally be prescribed until at least the age of 50, and possibly for a further eight to ten years. This is particularly true for women who have had a hysterectomy and can take pure oestrogen replacement therapy without the additional synthetic progestogen. Computer simulations suggest that taking all the risks and benefits into account, HRT is likely to prolong the life expectancy of a 50-year-old woman by up to a year. For a woman who has not had a hysterectomy, and who must take combined oestrogen and progestogen, the latter may cancel out some of the beneficial effects of the oestrogen replacement itself, although this is still under review.

What are the possible side effects?

Despite its health benefits, the use of HRT is still controversial. It is unfortunately linked with a number of side effects, including a possible increased risk of breast cancer. In most cases, the side effects of HRT are minor, occur at the start of treatment and settle down within a few weeks. Mild reactions are often helped by changing the dose or type of HRT you are taking. Patches, gels and creams, for example are usually associated with fewer side effects than oral tablets—because of the way these are absorbed into the bloodstream, they can contain lower doses. Possible side effects of HRT include:

nausea and vomiting	intolerance of contact lenses
breast tenderness and enlargement	skin reactions
breakthrough bleeding	loss of scalp hair
headache	increase in body or facial hair
dizziness	pre-menstrual syndrome
leg cramps or muscle pains	weight gain
increase in size of uterine fibroids	possible increased risk of breast cancer (see below)

It is also important to keep in contact with your doctor so that if unwanted side effects or unexpected problems do occur, you can discuss them and work out what is going on.

HRT should be stopped immediately and medical treatment sought if you develop:

- a first occurrence of migraine;
- frequent, severe headaches;
- sudden visual disturbances;
- signs of a blood clot (e.g. thrombophlebitis, thromboembolism) such as pain and swelling of a limb, poor circulation or discolouration of part of the body;
- rise in blood pressure;
- jaundice;
- pregnancy.

What about HRT and breast cancer?

Women who take HRT for 15 or more years may have an increased risk of breast cancer. Some research suggests the risk is as low as 0.07 per cent, while others suggest long-term use increases the risk by as much as 32 per cent.

It is now thought that HRT may trigger breast cancer earlier in women who *would have developed it anyway*. Because of the screening that occurs when you are on HRT, and because the cancer is likely to be picked up earlier than would otherwise have been the case, there is no evidence that taking HRT increases your risk of *dying* from breast cancer. In fact, women who use HRT before developing breast cancer may have a lower risk of death from breast cancer because stopping HRT causes a hormone-dependent tumour to shrink.

HRT should not be taken by women who:

- are pregnant or breast-feeding;
- have had an oestrogen-dependent cancer (e.g. of the breast) unless their doctor agrees—an increasing number of experts now feel that women who have been successfully treated for cancer and have no evidence of a recurrence can take HRT;
- have undiagnosed vaginal bleeding;
- have active endometriosis;
- have active blood-clotting disorders;
- have severe heart, liver or kidney disease.

It is only used with caution in women with a family history of breast cancer and those who have previously suffered from a blood-clotting problem (thromboembolism).

While some doctors recommend that HRT is stopped six weeks before major planned surgery, others no longer feel this is necessary for normal, low dose HRT—as long as heparin, a blood-thinning agent, is given after surgery.

NATURAL PROGESTERONE

Natural progesterone is gaining in popularity as a form of hormone replacement therapy. Like many synthetic hormones, it is derived from plants such as the wild yam (*Dioscorea villosa*) and soya bean. It is important to realise, however, that these creams do not contain extracts of wild yam or soya— several chemical changes are made to the steroid building blocks found in these plants to synthesise progesterone. It is labelled 'natural' as it is the same chemical structure as the progesterone naturally found in the human body, not because it is a natural extract. Natural progesterone cream is therefore just another form of hormone replacement therapy—in this case, progesterone replacement instead of the usual HRT combination of an oestrogen plus a progestogen.

Natural progesterone, as we have seen, cannot be given by mouth because it is quickly broken down in the gut. It is therefore given as a suppository or as a cream to be absorbed into the circulation through a mucous membrane or the skin. Some research suggests it does not pass from the skin into the bloodstream very well, however, and tends to accumulate in the underlying fat cells. Nevertheless, some experts believe that progesterone cream has a beneficial effect on bones to increase bone density. In one trial, post-menopausal women showed as much as a 10–25 per cent increase in bone mineral density after 12 months' treatment. It is important to point out that they were also advised to:

- include green leafy vegetables in their diet;
- exercise three times a week;
- reduce consumption of cigarettes, alcohol and red meat;
- take supplements of calcium, vitamin D and vitamin C.

Some also took oestrogen for three weeks per month if appropriate, although the effect of oestrogen plus progesterone cream was found not to be superior to progesterone cream (plus diet and lifestyle changes) without oestrogen.

The effects of progesterone cream alone are still under investigation. Certainly bone-building cells (osteoblasts) seem to have progesterone receptors just as they have oestrogen receptors. As yet, there are no long-term trials showing the benefits of progesterone in treating post-menopausal women. As a result, the Council of the British Menopause Society is concerned about the claims being made for natural progesterone products which have not been proven by properly controlled scientific studies. It states:

It has been well substantiated that oestrogen deficiency is a major factor in the development of menopausal symptoms, osteoporosis and cardiovascular disease in post-menopausal women. Properly controlled scientific trials reported in peer-review journals have confirmed the value of hormone replacement with naturally-occurring oestrogens ... We find claims for progesterone preparations particularly worrying. Although progesterone/progestogens may have some beneficial effects on hot flushes and bone density, there are not data provided on the amount of progesterone which is absorbed from these preparations.

Post-menopausal women should be reassured that [oestrogen] HRT remains the treatment of choice for menopausal symptoms, osteoporosis and cardiovascular disease and there is no scientific evidence to support a change to 'alternative' therapies ... The BMS has issued this statement in the hope that women will continue to seek informed advice from their medical practitioner or menopause clinic, and that those who are considering or currently taking HRT will not be easily dissuaded from obtaining the proven benefits of natural oestrogen replacement.

While oestrogen HRT should always be the first option considered for treatment of post-menopausal symptoms and for protection against osteoporosis and coronary heart disease, many women cannot take it or prefer not to do so. As natural progesterone has virtually no known ill-effects, and may well be beneficial in helping to protect against osteoporosis, it may be worth trying. Do continue with other measures such as dietary and lifestyle changes, however.

TESTOSTERONE

Testosterone is a male hormone (androgen) produced by the testicles. Testosterone is secreted continuously and, unlike levels of oestrogen in the female, does not peak and fall in a monthly cycle. Highest blood levels occur during the teens and early 20s and testosterone levels then gradually decrease. It now seems certain that some males experience a form of male menopause referred to as an andropause or viripause. Symptoms include tiredness, irritability, low sex drive, aching joints, dry skin, insomnia, excessive sweating, hot flushes and depression. In the long term, bone thinning may also occur in a manner similar to that affecting post-menopausal women. Between the ages of 40 and 70 years, male bone density falls by up to 15 per cent and men also lose an average of 5–10 kg in muscle weight. Sperm counts tend to drop and failure to achieve an erection occurs more frequently—all evidence that the testosterone hormone is failing to do its job.

Many men with these symptoms have a testosterone level that is within the normal range, however. Their symptoms may therefore be due to an interaction problem between testosterone and its receptors, or to excessive alcohol intake or high stress levels which increase the rate at which testosterone is broken down in the body. Another possibility is that the levels of the protein that binds sex hormones (sex hormone binding globulin or SHBG) are high. SHBG mops up free testosterone and inactivates it. Therefore, even though it is present and measurable in the bloodstream, the hormone cannot exert its usual effects. Male hormone replacement therapy (HRT) is available in the form of:

- pills given up to three times a day for three to six months;
- an implant, which is inserted into the buttock and slowly releases testosterone over a six-month period;
- an injection given every two to six weeks;
- a skin patch which is replaced every 24 hours.

Male HRT is still controversial and not many doctors will prescribe it. It is usually available only from a hormone specialist (endocrinologist) or male health specialist (andrologist) where there is proven underactivity of the testicles (hypogonadism) and low testosterone levels. Hypogonadism is found in up to 20 per cent of men with osteoporotic fractures of the spinal vertebrae, and up to 50 per cent of men with hip fractures. Testosterone replacement therapy helps to prevent osteoporosis by:

- boosting absorption of calcium and vitamin D from the gut;
- raising levels of oestradiol (men naturally have small circulating levels of oestrogen hormone);
- raising levels of calcitonin (a hormone that builds bone—see p.162)
- decreasing resorption of old bone;
- increasing production of new bone.

Increased levels of testosterone have been linked with cancer of the prostrate gland.

DHEA

DHEA (dehydroepiandrosterone) is one of the hormones produced by the adrenal glands. It is similar in structure to oestrogen, progesterone and testosterone, but has its own separate effects. It can also be converted into sex hormones when levels are low, acting as a sort of buffer hormone.

Your level of DHEA naturally falls with age. At the age of 20, you produce around 30mg per day, but this drops to less than 6mg daily after the menopause. Falling levels of DHEA have been linked with many effects of ageing, including increased risk of osteoporosis. It has been suggested that DHEA supplements might help to prevent osteoporosis as:

- it may stimulate calcium absorption;
- it may stimulate new bone formation;
- a breakdown product of DHEA (called 5-androstene-3ß, 17 ß-diol) can activate oestrogen receptors and mimic oestrogen effects on bone (i.e. preventing bone reabsorption);
- it can help to raise low levels of oestrogen, progesterone or testosterone but without increasing the risk of hormone-dependent cancers—indeed, it seems to protect against them.

It is thought that DHEA is the only hormone capable of both inhibiting resorption of old bone and increasing production of new bone. If this is the case, then DHEA could be used to both prevent and treat osteoporosis. Trials are currently under way in the USA. To date, research suggests that women with high natural levels of DHEA are less likely to develop osteoporosis than those with low levels.

DHEA supplements have also been shown to:
—increase energy levels
—boost sex drive
—improve immunity to disease (including cancer)
—reduce the adverse effects of stress
—enhance memory
—improve mental function
—lift depression
—decrease body fat percentage

—possibly extend life span

In the USA, DHEA is available over the counter and has spawned a multimillion dollar industry. It is not licensed for use in the UK but can readily be obtained by mail order from the USA (see Useful Addresses). It seems to be safe in doses from 3–30mg per day, which is the range usually recommended. Side effects such as acne, increased hair growth and mild abnormalities of sugar metabolism have been reported in high doses. One word of warning: as DHEA is a biological hormone that has not yet been fully researched, it may well have other effects in the body that have not yet come to light.

BIPHOSPHONATES

Biphosphonates (e.g. etidronate, alendronate) are drugs that help to protect against osteoporosis. They work by blocking the action of cells which break down old bone (osteoclasts) so that bone-building bones (osteoblasts) can keep up with them and build more new bone. They have been shown to:

- slow the rate at which bone is resorbed;
- stimulate production of new bone;
- reduce the risk of bone fracture.

As well as being used to treat established osteoporosis, biphosphonates are now also used to prevent osteoporosis in women at high risk. Research shows they can build up bones in the spine, wrist and hip to reduce the risk of a fracture in postmenopausal women by as much as 88 per cent.

Etidronate is given in 90-day cycles for two weeks every three months: etidronate for 14 days, followed by effervescent calcium carbonate tablets for 76 days. It is mainly active on the bones in the back to reduce the risk of vertebral osteoporotic fractures.

Alendronate is considered to be 100 times more powerful then etidronate. It is taken on a daily basis and strengthens all bones in the body to reduce the risk of spinal, wrist and hip fractures by 48–55 per cent. The risk of having two or more spinal fractures is reduced by as much as 90 per cent. Possible side effects include:

- abdominal pain and distension
- flatulence
- diarrhoea or constipation
- muscle and bone pain
- headache
- rash

Biphosphonates must be taken with a full glass of water on an empty stomach. Alendronate must be taken at least 30 minutes before breakfast, and etidronate at least two hours before or after food. You must then stand or sit upright for at least 30 minutes and not lie down until after eating breakfast. This is to ensure the tablet stays in the stomach, and does not come back up into the oesophagus (gullet) where it can cause inflammation and ulceration.

Researchers are currently testing a range of other biphosphonates, including one called tiludronate, to see if they can help prevent or treat osteoporosis.

CALCITONIN

Calcitonin is a hormone injection, originally derived from salmon but now made synthetically. It helps to regulate bone turn-over and increases bone density in women with osteoporosis. It is used to treat rather than prevent osteoporosis and works by suppressing resorption of calcium from old bone. It is given by daily injection together with calcium and vitamin D supplements.

SODIUM FLUORIDE

Sodium fluoride is occasionally used to treat established osteoporosis. It binds to bone tissue to increase its stability and reduce resorption. It also stimulates osteoblasts to build new bone, although the quality of this new bone is under question. One in three women treated with fluoride will develop stomach irritation (gastritis) and one in ten develop painful swelling of the ankles and heels.

THE FUTURE: SERMs

SERMs are a new class of drug, whose name stands for Selective Estrogen Receptor Mediators (using the American spelling for oestrogen). The first SERM, raloxifene, is currently under investigation for its beneficial protective effects against osteoporosis and coronary heart disease. Another, droloxifene, is also in the pipeline.

SERMs mimic the beneficial action of oestrogen on your bones and circulation while damping down oestrogen effects in your womb and breasts. A SERM can therefore protect against osteoporosis and coronary heart disease without increasing your risk of breast or womb cancer. It also has the advantage of not triggering menstrual spotting or bleeding. Once it is launched in the UK, it will be a major advance for women who are unable or unwilling to take traditional HRT because of its unwanted side effects.

Raloxifene significantly increases bone mineral density compared with the bone loss seen in similar women taking calcium and placebo.

POTASSIUM BICARBONATE

A dietary supplement, potassium bicarbonate, is currently under investigation for the prevention of osteoporosis. It is an alkaline salt commonly found in fruit and vegetables. It is thought to help protect against osteoporosis by neutralising excess acid created in the body as a result of a diet rich in animal products, especially meats. Excess acid is thought to leach calcium from the bones and increase bone loss in the urine to increase the risk of spinal and hip fractures.

When post-menopausal women were given regular potassium bicarbonate supplements, they were found to lose less calcium in their urine. They also seemed to form more bone and experience less bone loss. The results of the trial are expected in early 1998. In the meantime, continue eating more fruit and vegetables for their potassium bicarbonate content, as well as their other beneficial components: vitamins, minerals, trace elements, essential fatty acids and plant oestrogens.

PARATHYROID HORMONE

Parathyroid hormone (also known as parathormone) is a naturally occurring hormone made by the four parathyroid glands in the throat. Parathormone helps to control the amount of calcium in the blood and when given as a drug can help to build new bone and prevent—or treat—osteoporosis. Some research suggests that in high doses parathormone can completely restore bone density, even where it has been thinned by as much as 50 per cent. It is currently under trial in patients who have osteoporosis as a result of taking corticosteroid drugs. It is expected to increase bone density by 20–40 per cent which, if borne out, will be an exciting advance.

APPENDICES

FOODS HIGH IN CALCIUM
in mg per 100g (4oz approx.)

Grain products	*mg*
White bread with added fibre	150
French stick, white	130
Brown bread	110
Brown bread, toasted	140
Wheat bread flour, white	140
Wheatflour, brown	130
Muffins	140
Toasted crumpet	120
Yorkshire pudding	130
Muesli	200
Tortilla chips	150
Semi-sweet biscuits	120
Pasta	25–30

Milk and eggs	
Parmesan cheese	1200
Cheddar cheese, reduced fat	840
Cheddar cheese, English	740
Edam cheese	770
Mozzarella cheese	590
Brie	540
Feta cheese	360
Cottage cheese, plain	73
Chocolate, white	270
Chocolate, milk	220
Whole milk yoghurt, plain	200
Low fat yoghurt, plain	190

Low fat yoghurt, flavoured	150
Greek yoghurt	150
Fromage frais, plain	89
Dairy ice-cream, vanilla	140
Egg custard	130
Egg yolk	130
Milk, whole (average)	115
Milk, Channel Island whole	130
Milk, semi-skimmed	120
Milk, skimmed	120

Herbs and spices

Dill, fresh	340
Basil, fresh	250
Basil, dried	2110
Marjoram dried	1990
Thyme, fresh	630
Thyme, dried	1890
Sage, fresh	600
Sage, dried	1650
Oregano, fresh	310
Oregano, dried	1580
Mint, fresh	210
Parsley, fresh	200
Tarragon, fresh	170
Coriander leaves, fresh	98
Coriander seeds	660
Sunflower seeds	110
Poppy seeds	1580
Sesame seeds	620
Tahini paste	680
Curry powder	640
Pesto sauce	560
Black pepper	430
Rock salt (versus table salt)	230 (29)

Vegetables and pulses

Green beans, dried	350
Spring greens	210
Broccoli	200
Haricot beans, dried	180
Spinach	170
Watercress	170
Chickpeas, dried	160
Okra	160
Curly kale	150
Broad beans, dried	100
Red kidney beans, dried	100
Lentils, dried	71

Soya products

Tofu	1480
Soya bean curd	530

Fruit

Figs, dried	250
Figs (ready to eat)	230
Rhubarb	93
Apricots, dried	92
Apricots (ready to eat)	73
Olives	61
Oranges	47

Nuts

Almonds	240
Brazil nuts	170
Hazelnuts	140
Walnuts	94

Fish

Sardines, fresh	130
Sardines, canned	540
Shrimps	320
Prawns, boiled	110
Anchovies	300
Salmon, canned	300
Pilchards in tomato sauce	250
Fish cakes	150
Oysters	140
Sea bass, fresh	130
Plaice, fresh	130
Haddock	58

Meat

Premium sausages	180

FOODS HIGH IN MAGNESIUM
in mg per 100g (4oz approx.)

Grain products	*mg*
Wheatbran	520
Wheatgerm	270
Bulgar wheat	140
Wheatflour, wholemeal	120
Pasta, wholemeal, raw	120
Pasta, white	56
Wholemeal bread	80
Granary bread	59
Bran muffins	110
Muesli	100

Milk and eggs
Parmesan cheese   45

Herbs and spices
Thyme, fresh   73
Coriander leaves, dried   690
Coriander seeds   330
Cardamom, ground   230
Dill, fresh   44
Dill, dried   440
Sage, fresh   170
Sage, dried   430
Basil, dried   420
Oregano, fresh   53
Oregano, dried   270
Tarragon, fresh   51
Tarragon, dried   350
Sunflower seeds   390
Fennel seeds   390
Sesame seeds   370
Tahini paste   380
Cumin seeds   370
Poppy seeds   330
Pumpkin seeds   270
Curry powder   270
Black pepper   190
Rock salt (versus table salt)   140 (76)
Pesto sauce   69

Vegetables and pulses
Soya beans, dried   250
Soya beans, boiled   63
Butterbeans, raw   190
Broad beans, dried   190
Haricot beans, dried   190

Pinto beans, dried	190
Green beans, dried	160
Mung beans, dried	150
Red kidney beans, dried	150
Black eye beans, raw	140
Aduki beans, dried	130
Split peas, dried	130
Brown rice, raw	110
Brown rice, boiled	43
White rice, boiled	90
Spinach	54
Spinach, dried	470
Chickpeas, dried	110
Hummus	62
Lentils, dried	110
Okra	71

Fruit

Apricots, dried	65
Figs, dried	80
Figs (ready to eat)	73
Papaya	56

Nuts

Brazil nuts	410
Cashew nuts	270
Almonds	270
Pine nuts	270
Peanuts	210
Brazil nuts (weighed with shell)	190
Hazelnuts	160
Nut roast	110
Almonds	110
Walnuts	160

Fish

Shrimps, boiled	110
Prawns, boiled	48
White fish	62
Anchovies	56
Sardines	46

Sweetener

Molasses	240

FOODS HIGH IN ZINC
in mg per 100g (4oz approx.)

Grain products	*mg*
Wheatgerm	17
Wheat bran	16.2
Dried yeast	8
All-bran	6.7

Milk and eggs	
Parmesan cheese	5.3

Herbs and spices	
Chervil, dried	8.8
Basil dried	5.8
Thyme, dried	6.2
Poppy seeds	8.5
Pumpkin seeds	6.6
Sesame seeds	5.3
Tahini paste	5.5
Sunflower seeds	5.3

Vegetables and pulses
Spinach, dried   6.1

Nuts
Cashew nuts   5.9
Pecan nuts   5.4
Pine nuts   6.5

Fish
Oysters, raw   59.2
Whelks, boiled   12.1

Meat
Calves' liver   15
Lean steak   9.5
Lamb   6.1

FOODS HIGH IN VITAMIN D
in mcg per 100g (4oz approx.)

Fats and oils	*mcg*
Cod liver oil	210
Polyunsaturated margarine	8

Fish
Kipper   25
Salmon, fresh   10
Salmon, canned   23
Herring   19
Cod roe   18
Sardines, fresh   11
Pilchards in tomato sauce   14
Rainbow trout   11

APPENDICES

Mackerel, fresh   5
Mackerel, smoked   8
Tuna, fresh   7

Optimum Healthy Weight Range

HEIGHT		MEN			WOMEN	
Metres	*Feet*	*Kg*	*Stones*		*Kg*	*Stones*
1.47	4'10"				43–53	6st 10–8st 6
1.50	4'11"				43–55	6st 11–8st 9
1.52	5ft				45–56	7st 1–8st 11
1.55	5'1"				45–57	7st 1–8st 13
1.57	5'2"				46–59	7st 3–9st 4
1.60	5'3"				48–61	7st 8–9st 8
1.63	5'4"				50–63	7st 12–9st 13
1.65	5'5"				51–65	8st–10st 3
1.68	5'6"	56–70	8st 11–11st		53–67	8st 5–10st 7
1.70	5'7"	58–72	9st 1–11st 4		54–69	8st 7–10st 12
1.73	5'8"	60–75	9st 6–11st 11		56–71	8st 11–11st 2
1.75	5'9"	61–76	9st 8–12st		57–73	8st 13–11st 7
1.78	5'10"	63–79	9st 13–12st 6		59–75	9st 4–11st 11
1.80	5'11'	65–81	10st 3–12st 9		61–77	9st 8–12st
1.83	6ft	67–83	10st 7–13st 1		63–80	9st 13–12st 8
1.85	6'1"	69–85	10st 12–13st 5			
1.88	6'2"	71–88	11st 2–13st 12			
1.90	6'3"	72–90	11st 5–14st 2			
1.93	6'4"	75–93	11st 11–14st 8			

OPTIMUM HEALTHY WEIGHT RANGE

US EQUIVALENTS

MEN	WOMEN	
Feet	*Pounds*	*Pounds*
4'10"		*94–118*
4'11"		*95–121*
5ft		*99–123*
5'1"		*99–125*
5'2"		*101–130*
5'3"		*106–134*
5'4"		*110–139*
5'5"		*112–143*
5'6"	*123–154*	*117–147*
5'7"	*127–158*	*119–152*
5'8"	*132–165*	*123–156*
5'9"	*134–168*	*125–161*
5'10"	*139–174*	*130–165*
5'11"	*143–177*	*134–168*
6 ft	*147–183*	*139–176*
6'1"	*152–187*	
6'2"	*156–194*	
6'3"	*159–198*	
6'4"	*165–204*	

Sensible Weight Loss

Aim to lose weight by filling up on starchy foods, fruit and vegetables, cutting back on fats and sugary foods, as well as taking regular exercise:

- Breakfast like a king, lunch like a prince and dine like a pauper.
- Help yourself to slightly smaller portions and put them on a small plate.
- Eat more fresh fruit, vegetables and salads.
- Eat more oily fish.
- Fill up on foods rich in starch and fibre (e.g. baked

potatoes, brown rice, wholewheat pasta, wholegrain bread) but don't add fatty sauces.

- Drink at least 1 pint of skimmed or semi-skimmed milk per day.
- Use low fat products where possible.
- Cut back on meat and have one or two vegetarian days per week.
- Cut down on all fatty foods, including beefburgers, sausages, pies, pizza, crisps and chips.
- Cut down on sugary foods such as cakes, biscuits, doughnuts, pastries and confectionery.
- Take a good vitamin and mineral supplement plus evening primrose oil daily.

YOUR PERSONAL OSTEOPOROSIS RISK ANALYSIS

Are you at high risk of developing osteoporosis?

General

1 Increased risk of osteoporosis can be hereditary. Does osteoporosis run in your family?

YES [　] NO [　]

2 Smoking cigarettes significantly increases the risk of osteoporosis in later life. Have you smoked cigarettes for at least five years since the age of 45—or are you likely to?

YES [　] NO [　]

3 Heavy alcohol intake is known to increase your risk of osteoporosis. Do you regularly drink more than 2–3 units per day (women) or 3–4 units per day (men) or have you ever done so? (See p.13 for unit equivalents.)

YES [　] NO [　]

4 Using antacids containing aluminium for more than 10 years can double the risk of a hip fracture. Have you regularly used an antacid containing aluminium, or have you regularly eaten food cooked in aluminium saucepans?

YES [　] NO [　]

5 People who are underweight are at increased risk of osteoporosis. Are you underweight (BMI less than 19)? BMI = body weight (kg)/height (m)/height (m). (See p.10.)

YES [   ] NO [   ]

6 Taking oral corticosteroid drugs for more than three months increases your risk of future osteoporosis. Have you ever had to take long courses of oral corticosteroids?

YES [   ] NO [   ]

7 Some health problems are linked with an increased risk of osteoporosis. Do you suffer from kidney or liver disease?

YES [   ] NO [   ]

8 Do you suffer from problems with your thyroid or parathyroid glands?

YES [   ] NO [   ]

Exercise and Diet
9 Regular weight-bearing exercise is known to build up bones and help to prevent osteoporosis. Do you exercise *less* than five times per week on average?

YES [   ] NO [   ]

10 Have you ever had to take prolonged bed rest, especially in childhood?

YES [   ] NO [   ]

11 Excessive exercise increases your risk of osteoporosis. Have you ever been in intensive training as an athlete, for running a marathon, ballet dancing, etc?

YES [   ] NO [   ]

12 An adequate intake of dietary calcium is essential at all times of life to protect against future. Do you drink *less* than the equivalent of a pint of milk per day?

YES [   ] NO [   ]

13 Do you regularly eat white processed bread, rice, pasta, cereals rather than wholegrain (brown) products?

YES [ ] NO [ ]

14 Have you regularly gone without taking a vitamin and mineral supplement or only do so haphazardly?

YES [ ] NO [ ]

15 A high intake of fruit and vegetables has been shown to protect against osteoporosis. Do you eat *less* than five servings of fruit and vegetables per day?

YES [ ] NO [ ]

16 A diet rich in essential fatty acids has been shown to increase the calcium content of bones. Do you eat *less* than 300g oily fish (2–3 servings mackerel, herring, salmon, trout, sardines or pilchards) per week?

YES [ ] NO [ ]

17 Answer YES if you do not regularly consume sunflower, rapeseed, olive or nut oils, or evening primrose oil supplements.

YES [ ] NO [ ]

18 A high intake of salt is linked with an increased risk of osteoporosis. Do you regularly add salt during cooking or at the table, or eat salty foods such as crisps, salted nuts, etc?

YES [ ] NO [ ]

19 A high intake of caffeine is linked with an increased risk of osteoporosis. Do you have more than five caffeine-containing drinks per day?

YES [ ] NO [ ]

20 A high meat intake is linked with an increased risk of osteoporosis. Do you regularly eat meat once a day or more?

YES [　] NO [　]

21 Having an eating disorder can increase your risk of osteo-porosis. Have you ever suffered from anorexia or bulimia?

YES [　] NO [　]

Women only
22 Multiple child-bearing can increase your calcium loss from bones. Have you had more than two pregnancies?

YES [　] NO [　]

23 Have you breast-fed more than two babies?

YES [　] NO [　]

24 Have your periods ever stopped for more than six months for any reason other than pregnancy (e.g. depot forms of con-traception in which hormones are implanted under the skin, excessive weight loss or exercise, hormone imbalances)?

YES [　] NO [　]

25 Experiencing an early menopause before the age of 45 years increases your risk of osteoporosis. Have you had an early menopause, or does this run in your family?

YES [　] NO [　]

26 Have you had a hysterectomy and removal of both ovaries?

YES [　] NO [　]

27 Hormone replacement therapy (HRT) reduces the risk of hip fracture by up to 40 per cent after seven years' use, even in women with established osteoporosis. Answer YES if you are not currently using HRT, would not consider using it in the future, or are unable to take it.

YES [　] NO [　]

Score 1 point for every YES answer. Total =

YOUR PERSONAL OSTEOPOROSIS RISK ANALYSIS

Every YES answer that you give increases your risk of osteoporosis. Make as many changes to your diet and life-style as you can, but if you are worried by your increased risk of osteoporosis, seek medical advice.

USEFUL ADDRESSES

UK ADDRESSES

National Osteoporosis Society
PO Box 10, Radstock, Bath, BA3 3YB.
Helpline: 01761 472721 (9.30am–4.30pm)

Menopause and HRT

Amarant Trust
Grant House, 56–60 St John Street, London EC1M 4DT.
Tel: 0171-490-1644 Premium-rate helpline: 0891-660620
Aims to promote a better understanding of the menopause and HRT, and to make treatment available to all women who need it. Voluntary self-help groups throughout the UK.

Nutrition

Women's Nutritional Advisory Service
PO Box 268, Lewes, Sussex BN7 2QN.
Tel: 01273 487366
Advice and nutritional information for treating menopausal symptoms and osteoporosis (a fee is payable).

Eating for Pregnancy Helpline: 0114 2424084

Efamol (evening primrose oil) information line:
 01483 570248.

USEFUL ADDRESSES

Alcohol

National Alcohol Helpline:
Drinkline: 0171-332 0202 (London only).
0345 320202 (nationwide) All calls charged at local rates.
Dial and listen: 0500 801 802 FREECALL.

Alcohol Concern
Waterbridge House, 32–36 Loman Street, London SE1 0EE.
Tel: 0171-928-7377
Information service.

Smoking

QUIT
102 Gloucester Place, London W1H 3DA.
Smokers' Quitline: 0171-487-3000 (09.30 – 17.30 daily).
Advice and counselling on giving up smoking.

Logado (aromatherapy device) Consumer Advice Line:
01223 426410.

Complementary Therapies

British Acupuncture Association and Register
34 Alderney Street, London SW1V 4EU.
Tel: 0171-834-1012
Information leaflets, booklets, register of qualified practitioners.

British Herbal Medicine Association
Sun House, Church Street, Stroud GL5 1JL.
Tel: 01453 751389
Information leaflets, booklets, compendium, telephone advice.

British Homoeopathic Association
27A Devonshire Street, London W1N 1RJ.
Tel: 0171-9352163 (1.30-5.30 pm)
Leaflets, referral to medically qualified homoeopathic doctors.

General Council and Register of Naturopaths
Frazer House, 6 Netherall Gardens, London NW3 5RR.
Tel: 0171-435-8728

International Stress Management Association
The Priory Hospital, Priory Lane, London SW15 5JJ.
Tel: 0181-876-8261
Information on stress management and control. Leaflets, booklets, counselling.

Society of Teachers of the Alexander Technique
20 London House, 266 Fulham Road, London SW10 9EL.
Tel: 0171 351 0828

Suppliers

Body Treats
Tel: 0181 543 7633.
For tarragon essential oil.

Natural by Nature Oils
Tel: 0181 202 5718.
For star anise essential oil.

Bioelectromagnetic patches available from:
Tel: 0121 236 2073.

US ADDRESSES

Office on Smoking and Health
National Center for Chronic Disease Prevention, US Department of Health and Human Services, 1600 Clifton Road NE, Atlanta, GA 30333.

National Osteoporosis Foundation
2100 M Street, NW, Washington, DC 20037.
Tel: 202 223 2226

Women's Sports Foundation
Eisenhower Park, East Meadow, NY 11554.
Tel: 516 542 4700. Fax 516 542 4716

American Heart Association
7272 Greenville Avenue, Dallas, TX 75231
Tel: 214 373 6300

American Anorexic/Bulimia Association
165 West 46th Street, 1108 New York, NY 10036.
Tel: 212 575 6200

National Clearinghouse for Alcohol and Drug Information
PO Box 2345, Rockville, MD 20847-2345.
Tel: 301 468 2600 or 800 662 4357

National Women's Health Resource Center
Suite 325, 2440 M St NW, Washington DC 20037.
Tel: 202 293 6045

National Women's Health Network
514 10th Street NW, Suite 400, Washington DC 20004.
Tel: 202 347 1140

Native American Women's Health Education Resource Center
PO Box 572, Lake Andes, SD 57356.
Tel: 605 487 7072. E-mail: komanche@charles-mixcom

Society for Nutrition Education
2850 Metro Drive, Suite 416, Minneapolis, MN 55425.
Tel: 612 854 0035

American Association of Naturopathic Physicians
PO Box 20386, Seattle, WA 98112.

American Institute of Homeopathy
1585 Glencoe Street, #44, Denver, CO 80220.
Tel: 303 370 9164

American Academy of Medical Acupuncture
5820 Wilshire Boulevard, Suite 500, Los Angeles, CA 20036.
Tel: 880 521 2262

Life Enhancement Products Ltd.
PO Box 751390, Petaluma, CA 94975-1390.
Tel: 707 762 6144. Fax: 707 769 8016.
Suppliers of DHEA supplements.

Index

acupuncture 100–1
alcohol 8–9, 10, 12–16
Alexander technique 101
alfalfa 91
aluminium antacids 19–20
aromatherapy 19, 99–100

bioelectromagnetic therapy 101–3
biphosphonates 161–2
black cohosh 91–2
boron 58–9

caffeine 54
calcitonin 162
calcium 59–62, 85–6
chiropractic 103
comfrey 92
copper 63–4

diet 53, 55–6
dietary fibre *see* fibre
DHEA (dehydroepiandrosterone) 159–61
dong quai 92–3

essential fatty acids 45–8, 87–8
exercise: 29–41
    and stress relief 23–7

false unicorn 93
fibre 49–50

fluoride 64–5
folic acid 75–7

ginseng 94–5

herbalism 90–7
homoeopathy 97–9
HRT (hormone replacement therapy) 151–5

liquorice 95

magnesium: 65–6
    required during pregnancy 86
manganese 66–7
male HRT 159
    see also testosterone
minerals 58–71, 85–6

natural plant oestrogens 42–5
natural progesterone 156–8
naturopathy 104
nutritional therapy 104

oestrogenic herbs *see* herbalism
osteopathy 104

parathyroid hormone 164
pfaffia 95–6
phosphrus: 54–5
    for bone health 67–8
phyto-oestrogen *see* natural plant oestrogens

phyto-progesterones *see* natural plant oestrogens
phytotherapy *see* herbalism
potassium bicarbonate 164
pregnancy 9, 82–3
protein 50–2, 87

roughage *see* fibre
red clover 96
recipes:
　meat dishes 133–9
　　lamb curry 138–9
　　lamb lasagne 136–7
　　Mediterranean moussaka 137–8
　　orange chicken with walnuts and herbs 135
　　roast rosemary lamb with cannellini beans 135–6
　　spicy chicken with lemon and olives 134–5
　　tarragon chicken 133–4
　miscellaneous 107–8
　　fruit and nut seed muesli 107
　　kedgeree 108
　　mixed seeds and nuts to sprinkle on salads 107
　pasta 146–9
　　with fennel and mixed Mediterranean herbs 147
　　with pesto 146
　　with smoked salmon and fennel 148
　　with tomato and mozzarella sauce 148
　　with tomato, tuna and basil sauce 149

　　with walnuts and coriander 147
　salads and starters 111–21
　　aromatic bean salad 115
　　bean and fennel salad 116
　　crab, olive, sesame and pine nut salad 117
　　flashed oysters with lemon, garlic and herbs 119–20
　　flashed oysters with yoghurt and breadcrumbs 120
　　Greek salad 112
　　green lentil, ginger and coriander salad 112–13
　　grilled Jerusalem artichokes with feta cheese 119
　　marinaded herring salad 118
　　Mediterranean bean salad 115
　　mixed leaf salad with feta cheese and hazelnuts 111–12
　　pasta salad with apple, cheese, celery, walnuts and grapes 116–17
　　pesto rice salad 117
　　salad niçoise 113–14
　　salmon tartare 120–1
　　tuna and pasta salad 114
　　walnut and coriander pâté 118–19
　sauces, dips and dressings 108–11

INDEX

Greek almond and garlic relish 109
hummus 111
Italian olive relish 110
pesto sauce 108–9
raita 110
walnut sauce 109
seafood 125–33
    baked orange and rosemary trout 130
    baked whole fish with lemon and herbs 125–6
    bouillabaisse 126–7
    grilled fish steaks with lemon and herbs 126
    grilled trout with walnuts and dill 130
    mackerel with ginger and fennel 128–9
    mackerel with mustard and herbs 128
    Mediterranean herb oil 125
    mixed seafood in tomato, fennel and chilli sauce 127–8
    moules marinières 132–3
    mussels stuffed with coriander, walnuts and cheese 133
    salmon in dill sauce 131
    sardines from Crete 129
    sea bass with fennel 131
    trout with almonds 129–30
    white fish with walnut sauce 132
soups 121–4

garlic and sesame croutons 121
Jerusalem artichoke and hazelnut soup 123
lentil and apricot soup 124
Mediterranean bean soup 121–2
Mediterranean fish soup 122–3
mushroom, garlic and fennel soup 124
vegetarian dishes 139–46
    aubergine and spinach with basil and walnuts 142–3
    aubergines parmesan 141
    cheese and lentil herb loaf 143–4
    green herbed omelette 139
    Mediterranean chickpeas 145–6
    Mediterranean fennel bake 145
    ratatouille 139–40
    roasted red pepper devils 140
    stuffed cinnamon aubergines 141–2
    walnut and mushroom nut roast 144–5

sage 96–7
salt 52–3
saturated fats 48–9
SERMs (selective estrogen receptor mediators) 163
silicon 68–9
smoking 8, 10, 16–19

sodium fluoride 163
stress 20—7
strontium 69—70
sugar 54
sunlight 11—12
supplements 80—1

t'ai-chi chu'an 104
testosterone 158—9

vitamins:
   for bone health 71—81
   recommended intake of
     83—4

vitamin A 72—3
vitamin B12 74—5
vitamin B6 73—4
vitamin C 77—8
vitamin D 78—9
   see also sunlight
vitamin K 79—80

water 55

yoga 105

zinc 70—1